T A L K

Teaching Adults to Lead Their Kids

*Talking to Your Children About Sex
and Other Things*

Frederica R. Jones

Cartoons by Chris Varricchione, http://www.cvillustration.com.

Editing by Debra O'Brien, debra4obrien@gmail.com.

The anecdotes in this book are true but the names have been changed in most cases to protect the anonymity of those who have shared their stories.

ISBN: 978-0-9885565-0-8

Admont Publishing - www.admontpublishing.com

1234R

DEDICATION

To Matthew, Kirsten, Andrew and Isaac whose parents are doing such a great job in talking with each of you. You are such a joy to know. I love you. Thank you for letting me be such a vital part of your lives.

CONTENTS

ACKNOWLEDGMENTS

This book is the result of a journey taken over the past 20 plus years and there are so many, many people who have encouraged me either through their enthusiasm during the workshops or in their testimonials of how this information has been so helpful in their parenting.

Thank you to Jill Gilmartin who, about 20 years ago, suggested the acronym TALK. This title has so aptly fit what I am trying to communicate.

I want to thank Lynn Marcott, professor of English at Gordon College, for pushing me toward the idea of writing this book by suggesting a writer's workshop and being a constant cheerleader whenever we talk.

Thanks to Julie Holliday whose shining eyes and enormous enthusiasm fueled my energies when I felt discouraged.

I want to thank Mike Yorkey, former editor of *Focus on The Family* magazine who greatly encouraged me after spending some time listening to my idea and reading some of what I had written. I still remember his words: "I have to tell many people that they do not have a good idea—you do. Write the book."

And to my very good friend Katie Griffin whose ear was always available, who was a constant source of support. Katie, you gave me so many ideas and were always so attentive to my thoughts—then you'd put them into action and come back to tell me the outcome. I am awed by your motherly persistence—your efforts show.

Chris Varricchione, thank you for your contribution to this book effort with your superlative cartoons; they add so much in illustrating various ideas. Thank you!

Thank you Emily Jones for being "fresh eyes," reading and giving helpful feedback on the proof copy of TALK. Your suggestions and comments were very helpful. Thank you so much for your time—particularly during a very busy season of the year.

Emily and Sarah, one could not have more wonderful daughters-in-law. You two are like a tag team—one or the other always ready to give me affirmation, to tell me about your successes in talking with your children, to cheer me on when I got fatigued. Thank you, Christopher, for technical help, for being a steady rock behind Emily as you parent those wonderful children—our grandchildren, and for your care, concern and love for me.

David, what a patient listener and huge source of encouragement you have been to me. Your words and love have meant so very much to me throughout this project. Thank you! Thank you for setting me on a solid course as I began to write and for always being interested in how it was going. Thanks for reading through my first stumbling attempts, then several iterations after that, and thank you for your encouragement to find a good editor.

Thank you, Debbie O'Brien, for being that editor. I could not have done this without your help! We became a team. Thank you for your untold hours of working over this manuscript. You have eagle eyes, seeing, even from a distance, when there were too many spaces or the font was off. You have taken my mumbled attempts to communicate through rather confusing sentences and paragraphs and turned them into eloquence! Your friendship, encouragement and labor on this project have been of inestimable value. What a gift you have been to me. Thank you sounds so inadequate—but indeed I do thank you for your tireless efforts. You have contributed in a major way to taking this work and making it worthy of public presentation.

And to my ever-patient, loving, supportive chief cheerleader—my husband, Brian—without you backing me steadily through this entire past year I would never have started nor would I have persevered. Thanks for taking on meal preparation, being a sounding board, listening to me talk thoughts out, reading through sections again and again and finally reading through the final drafts. Your comments have always been spot-on! Thank you also for the major effort on cover design and technical help—when I was ready to throw the computer out, you laid hands on it and solved the myriad problems. And all of this while you maintained your own work schedule, always having several balls in the air. Thank you for walking with me as we practiced the ideas put forth in this book in raising our two wonderful sons. What a joy to experience the ever deepening relationships that have developed through the years of their childhood, their courtships, marriages and now parenting. Thank you for loving me as Christ loves His church.

INTRODUCTION

After many years working as a registered nurse in pediatrics, public health and research, I "retired" to raise our two sons. When they were approaching middle school age, my husband and I decided to move from California to a small town in Vermont. Shortly after we moved, the community became embroiled in a discussion with the school district about the content to be taught in the health curriculum. The concern was that many parents did not want sex discussed in the public school classroom where it would be taught without regard for the moral standards of many homes. I later discovered that many of these same parents, however, were not discussing the subject in their homes.

I joined with a group of concerned parents who studied the issue. The outcome was a research paper which was presented to several parent and community groups and finally to the superintendent of our district. As a result of our research the district formed a parent advisory committee to work with the school board and I was named as one of the members of this committee. We worked together for about a year following which I was appointed to the faculty of one of the middle schools to teach health education.

I taught students in 5th through 8th grade for five years. At the conclusion of every class I sent home a flyer called "The Health Times." In it I would describe exactly what I taught in class and give some interactive questions for parent and student discussion. I also taught several parent classes, during my tenure, which were designed to answer parent questions and teach parents how to talk with their children. All of this in an effort to encourage communication in the home.

The Cycle of Silence

During this time I became increasingly convinced that many parents were not talking to their children about sex. Some demonstrated a fair amount of ignorance about puberty as well as anxiety about how to talk. If they tried, they often reported their children to be uncommunicative about the subject. The challenge was to develop techniques to break the cycle of silence, encouraging parents to talk early and often, laying the moral foundations they wanted for their children and arming them with a moral filter through which school teaching about sex would pass.

After I resigned from that teaching position I worked for about a year putting together a parent workshop entitled TALK: Teaching Adults to Lead Their Kids. Over the last 20 years I have given this workshop to parents in schools and churches in New England, New Jersey and Geneva, Switzerland. I have gleaned many stories of successes and failures from parents and have continued to research the issues involved. Parents have repeatedly responded positively to this workshop and urged me to put it into a book. You are holding in your hands that book: TALK.

Following are a sample of parents' comments about the workshop, the contents of which are in this book:

> ➢ "If you find yourselves at a loss to explain questions your children ask about sexuality or would like to make the most of 'teachable

moments' TALK is invaluable. It rouses you from reacting passively to being prepared and even anxious to have the relationship Freddie describes with your kids."

➤ "If parents could invest only four hours of their time to enhance their relationship with their children, TALK would be a wise investment."

➤ "I am willing to bet all parents, even the most experienced, could gain some benefit from TALK."

➤ "I really enjoyed TALK. It gave me great insight into my children's behavior in their teenage years and many valuable thoughts to take home and try out."

➤ "Very useful information, both from some of the amazing statistics to the interesting examples; it was fun, informative and a great encouragement to get started on this topic with my kids."

➤ "It is better to be prepared with your answers when the questions come from your children. TALK certainly gets you in good position for that!"

➤ "TALK hits the issues head on that are important to parent/child relationships and gives you the tools to deal with them."

➤ "One of the benefits of TALK was receiving reinforcement for things I had been doing well."

➤ "You will be encouraged as a parent not to be silent but to teach your values. They not only matter but are important to convey to our children even if we as parents aren't perfect..." (paraphrased).

➤ "It's wonderful to know how to approach your child with confidence and openness."

> ➤ "If you love your children you will be open and transparent. Learn how to feel comfortable doing so."
> ➤ "TALK was valuable and made me think that waiting too long to speak with our children could hurt them."
> ➤ "I wish I knew about TALK 10 years ago!"

What to Expect in This Book

In Section One we'll look at "The Problem": kids want parents to talk about sex but many parents are not talking. We'll explore *why* it is a problem when parents don't talk to their children about sex and some of the many reasons they don't. We'll also look at why it helps to talk and who *is* talking.

Section Two will discuss how to get started and how to keep the topic open. Then we'll deal with the many topics to be discussed as children grow toward adulthood. These topics are separated by chapters: preschool, elementary, middle school, high school and post high school years.

In Section Three we'll investigate the question, "Why would a good God design us for sex to be used only in marriage between a man and a woman?"

The need to be real and honest with our children will take us through Section Four. If we're not honest with our children, how can we expect them to be honest with us?

And finally, Section Five will look at the joy and hope parents can set before their children as they become adults.

Understanding the Problem

Chapter 1

THE PROBLEM

What is the problem? Simply stated, the problem is that kids want their parents to talk to them about sex and parents aren't talking.[1] When asked who they want to talk to them about sex, again and again adolescent students state: "We want our parents to talk to us."[2]

Nevertheless, parents are not talking. Parents often state that they want to talk with their kids about sex but they don't know how. They don't know when to begin. They don't know what's appropriate. They don't know how much is too much. And, as their children grow older, they don't know how to break down the wall of silence often erected by their adolescent sons and daughters. Parents all too often believe the spoken or unspoken message from their teens: "What you think (mom/dad) is irrelevant to my life." And so parents are silent on the subject of sex.

Even though silent, parents are not ignorant of the media overload that today's culture presents. They know only too well that their kids are in constant communication with their peers. They know that kids are quite curious about sex. They know the compromising moral standards of many around them and, though concerned about protecting their children, they are not talking with them about sexuality.

An article on MSNBC in early February 2012 reported on an inappropriate recess game played at a Minnesota Elementary School called "Rape Tag." When a student was tagged, they had to remain "frozen" until freed by someone climbing on top of them and simulating the sex act (humping). The school authorities dealt with this as soon as it came to their attention, seeing that it didn't continue. Letters were sent home to inform parents and suggest that they talk with their children about this game. About 15 to 20 parents contacted the school, "some of whom were upset about having to discuss the sensitive topic with their children."[3] Clearly, these parents had not talked with their children about sensitive topics when they were young and, now that their children were in elementary school, the parents were upset at the thought of having to address this topic. The longer parents wait to talk about sex, the harder it becomes. Consider Bob's story.

Bob grew up in a typical American home where his parents modeled a strong marriage. They were a close family, but his parents were silent on the subject of sex just as their parents had been. They did, however, have some understanding that parents needed to have "the talk" when their children approached dating age. Because Bob was a son, mom and dad agreed "the talk" was in the father's ball park. Therefore, dad geared himself up and, with not a small amount of dread, drove to their church on a Sunday evening to pick his son up from youth group.

Bob's father was noticeably nervous as he transferred the operation of the car to his son. It was a silent ride home. Tension could be felt in the car.

It was not until they drove into the darkened garage that Bob's father uncharacteristically laid his hand on his son's leg and said,

"Son, we need to talk about the birds and the bees."

"Aw, Dad," said Bob, "I know all about that."

"Good," said Bob's dad.

End of conversation. The tragedy was that Bob knew nothing about "the birds and the bees." One thing he did know: from his earliest memory, sex was a topic not discussed in his family. He had been shut down so many times that he knew the subject generated great embarrassment, discomfort, and was a topic completely shrouded in mystery and shame. Why talk to his dad about it now?

Children often want something that parents aren't giving. There is nothing new about this, but the question remains: Is it a problem that parents are not talking about sex with their children? The answer: Yes, and too much is at stake today to remain silent about this subject.

This is not a new problem. Ask any group of adults if their parents talked with them about sex or ask any group of grandparents and mostly you'll get shaking heads—"No." So, is talking important? Yes! It has always been important. But in today's world the stakes are much higher than they were sixty years ago.

The Moral Tsunami of the 1960s

The marketing of the birth control pill in the 1960s brought on a moral tsunami totally unexpected by the parents of that generation. It was silent, unanticipated, and resulted in devastating consequences. With the pill came a sexual revolution, a burgeoning of sexual experimentation termed "free love." But instead of freedom, the sexual revolution resulted in an increase in the frequency and variety of sexually transmitted diseases, diminishing sexual satisfaction, increasing loneliness, and escalating divorce rates. Painfully, it has been discovered that sex decoupled from committed relationship is not free.

Pre-1960

Even though parents weren't talking before 1960 any more than they are talking today, a societal consensus prevailed: sex is for marriage. Young people still slept with their boy/girlfriends, but these relationships usually progressed to marriage. Promiscuity was rare.

Post-1960

Since the moral tsunami of the 1960s, the resulting cultural changes have ravaged and continue to destroy, separate and disintegrate the American family. Consider how much the moral fabric of the culture has changed.

- ➢ Increases in sexually transmitted diseases
- ➢ Increases in single-parent families
- ➢ Increases in children born out of wedlock
- ➢ Increases in number of sexual partners
- ➢ Increases in teenage suicide rate
- ➢ Increases in availability of pornography

Let's explore these in detail starting with the increases in sexually transmitted diseases.

THE PROBLEM

Sexually Transmitted Diseases (STD's)

Before the 1960s, those at risk of sexually transmitted diseases faced contracting two varieties: gonorrhea and syphilis. Since the 1960s, many sexually transmitted diseases have been identified. The World Health Organization states that those who are sexually active now face the possibility of contracting more than 30 different sexually transmitted diseases,[4] with more being discovered all the time. (In some reports the number is closer to 60.) A Planned Parenthood spokesperson suggests that because there are so many sexually transmitted diseases and infections, half of us will get infected at some point in our lives.[5] Some of these diseases are insidiously silent. Chlamydia, for example, often produces no symptoms, yet it can cause infertility, chronic pain, or a tubal pregnancy if left untreated.

The infections are widespread and often invisible. "Many of the people who are transmitting these diseases are not symptomatic...," states Dr. Cohen, Director of the Institute of Global Health and Infectious Diseases.[6] These diseases were first called venereal diseases, then sexually transmitted diseases, and now are termed sexually transmitted *infections,* because they can be spread by a person who has no symptoms. The infected person may not even know they are infected. But even if a person knows they have a disease, with the privacy laws today, a person's sexual partner(s), even a spouse, will not be informed. It used to be that when a person was diagnosed with a sexually transmittable disease, a history of all contacts was taken. All contacts were sought out to be told that they may have been exposed. No more. This information is now "private" and none of those at risk for infection will be alerted. This is true even if HIV (the AIDS virus) is

7

the infection. Sexually transmitted diseases and infections are ravaging today's youth. But don't lose hope!

Single-Parent Families

In 1965, 10% of children in the United States were living in single-parent families. This percentage climbed to 29% by 1997[7], and by 2010 34% of children in the United States were living in single-parent households.[8]

Children Born out of Wedlock

Of babies born in 1940, only 3.8% were born out of wedlock.[9] Whereas in 2009, 41% of babies born in the United States were born to unwed mothers.[10] These statistics show that between 1940 and 2006 there was a huge increase in the number of babies born out of wedlock in the United States.

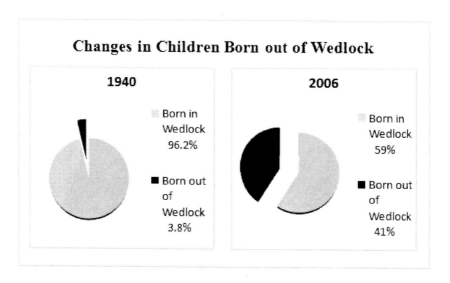

Number of Sexual Partners (Teens)

In earlier generations teens did not have multiple sexual partners. We know this because sexually transmitted diseases were not rampant. Multiple partners is what has caused the numbers and new types of sexually transmitted infections to spread rapidly and widely.

In 2008, about 40% of sexually active persons aged 15 to 19 had multiple sexual partners. This proportion increases with age. About 75% of sexually active persons aged 20 to 24 have multiple sexual partners. The younger the age of first intercourse, the greater the number of sex partners a person is apt to have in a lifetime.[11]

Teenage Suicide Rates

The teenage suicide rate has been increasing from that recorded in the middle of the 20th century until it has become the third leading cause of death in young people aged 15-24. Of particular note is the difference in the attempted suicide rate in virginal girls compared to non-virginal girls aged 12-16. The study was reported in 1991 in the *Journal of Pediatrics:* 6.9% of virginal girls had attempted suicide, compared to 31.9% of non-virginal girls.[12] Other statistics of note:

> ➤ "Between the mid-1950s and the late 1970s, the suicide rate among U.S. males aged 15-24 more than tripled (from 6.3 per 100,000 in 1955 to 21.3 in 1977). Among females aged 15-24, the rate more than doubled during this period (from 2.0 to 5.2 per 100,000)."[13]

> ➤ The National Youth Violence Prevention Resource Center found that 1 in 5 high school students thought about suicide, 1 in 6 students made plans for suicide, and more than 1 in 12 students attempted suicide.[14] One of the main factors listed for suicide in this age group was a recent loss, such as a romantic break up.[15]

Pornography Before and After the Internet

Before the Internet made the privacy of homes the place where pornography was accessed and viewed, accessing pornography necessitated going to an Adult Book Store or to the back room in the video store. Most people were reticent to do this because they feared that someone they knew might see what they were doing. One could always subscribe to magazines, but few sharing a home with their family wanted to be that obvious. After the Internet became available in the majority of homes, viewing pornography became an ultra-private behavior, and the numbers of those viewing pornography has since ballooned.

> ➤ Recent statistics report that 28,258 Internet users are viewing pornography *every second!*[16]
> ➤ Pornography is a 97-billion-dollar business worldwide.[17] Take that money and distribute it: you could give $48.50 to every man, woman, and child on the planet.
> ➤ In 2008 a study reported in the *Journal of Adolescent Research* stated that 87% of young men and 31% of young women aged 18-26 reported using pornography. The study also indicated that those

viewing pornography reported (1) having more sexual partners within the past year, compared to nonusers, and (2) being more accepting of non-marital cohabitation.[18]

The enormity of this problem cannot be overstated: pornography reaches into a huge number of homes. Christian homes are not exempt, and those who are bitten often become addicted. (See Chapter 7 for more on this problem.) The hope for taming this blight lies in the upcoming generation: parents helping their children to stay away from this danger by monitoring, talking, and always being on the alert. Don't think this can't happen to your children. Be aware of how insidious this problem is and how tempting to the curiosity of young adolescents. Be prepared to help them.

It is not a question of whether your children will be exposed to pornography—they will. The question is, what are you going to do about it?

Chapter 2

WHY AREN'T PARENTS TALKING?

Kids are looking for guidance to help navigate today's social minefields but finding their parents silent. Even from the time they begin to talk, they are asking questions. So why aren't parents talking to their children about sex? Consider the many and varied reasons.

Ignorance of Human Developmental Stages

Because today's parents have not had parents who talked with them about sex, they may have limited exposure to accurate information. They may not remember much of any teaching about reproductive parts and functions. What they don't know can't be imparted to their children. It could be a matter of simple ignorance.

Lack of Personal Modeling

Few of us have had parents who talked to us about sex so it just hasn't been modeled for us. We tend to have smaller families today and so can't use our own situations of pregnancy and breast feeding as starting points for conversations with our kids. Furthermore, few of us live on farms where children see birth among the animals, allowing obvious openings for conversations.

Confusion

Parents labor under many misconceptions regarding the topic of sex and how to communicate about it with their children. The following are some of the areas of confusion that parents have expressed:

Privacy vs. Pornography

The way the subject of sex is intentionally and carefully avoided, one might think that it was pornographic and not simply private. Pornography is defined as anything which is intended to cause sexual arousal. When parents talk to their children about sex and sexuality, the subject matter is absolutely not presented with the intention of sexual arousal. It is simply a subject which is private, something families talk about in their homes.

Private vs. Public

In the culture of talk shows, Facebook, Myspace, and other social media, there is confusion about what is private—to be talked about in our homes with those most connected to us—and what is appropriate for public discussion. People all too often blatantly share the most intimate details of their lives, including sexual struggles, on talk shows with people who really don't care, and yet never share their feelings and struggles with their spouse, children, or parents.

Innocence vs. Ignorance

Does anyone really want their children to be ignorant? No, it's innocence we're after. Jesus tells His disciples to "...be wise as serpents and innocent as doves" (Matthew 10:16b).

We want our children to have accurate and adequate information so they will be equipped to make wise choices that will maintain their innocence. Wisdom has to do with what we understand. Innocence has to do with behavior. The Apostle Paul puts it this way: "...I want you to be wise as to what is good and innocent as to what is evil" (Romans 16:19b).

Romantic vs. Illicit

In a newspaper article about sexually active teens, they were asked why they were sexually active before marriage. One 18-year-old was quoted: "I want to get my fun over with first."

Susan read this article to her high school-aged son who was interested in a young woman (later to become his wife). Because he intended to remain a virgin until he married, he responded to the article:

"Well, I guess I'll just have to give up romance."

"Do you really think that all romance is illicit?" Susan challenged. "Do you think you can't be romantic without being physical? Do you think you can't be married and be romantic?"

Her son rather sheepishly acknowledged that fun and romance need not necessarily be coupled with sex.

Inaccurate Assumptions

Parents labor under many inaccurate assumptions. Either they have been told, or in their attempts to skirt their responsibility, they claim some of the following:

My Child Is Too Young

"I'll get to 'the talk' later." Research, on the other hand, states the earlier the better. A mother of a ten-year-old asked: "My daughter appears to be approaching puberty. When should I have 'the talk?'" Answer: About ten years ago, and not "the talk," but continuous dialogue. "According to experts, the preschool years are the ideal, even essential, time to begin talking to your child about sex and sexuality."[19]

The Chicken or the Egg

Another inaccurate assumption resembles the chicken or the egg question: Which comes first? Many parents think, "If my child wants to know, he'll ask." Research indicates, instead, that he/she stopped asking because you made it quite clear that you don't want to talk about it.

The following is an example of a mom who thought that, since she and her daughter talked all the time, her daughter would ask if she wanted to know about sex. The mom had attended a TALK workshop where one of my suggestions was that she read her daughter an age-appropriate book which talked about puberty development and the way our bodies are designed. She immediately bought one and did so. Here is her comment from an e-mail:

I had a few "good long" conversations with [my 10-year-old daughter] which has really set the stage for a great work. I feel...the link of trust is better established and she is now totally comfortable talking about the subject (these are actually her own words...). It was interesting for me to see because...we always talked about everything so *I naively assumed she would talk about it when needed...but she was afraid to bring up the subject...* (emphasis added).

Lack of Relationship

In today's fast-paced world, relationships often suffer. The myriad time-saving devices in our homes seem to make little difference—there's never enough time. And time is needed to build relationships. Because poor parent-child relationships can have dangerous consequences in the area of teenage sexuality, relationship-building needs to become a renewed priority within our homes.

Respect, trust, and relationship are closely related. Both respect and trust are an outgrowth of a positive relationship where people are consistently honest and humble. With that kind of a relationship we can be real, we can be ourselves, we don't have to cover our faults, we can freely forgive and ask forgiveness, and we're usually given the benefit of the doubt. In the context of a healthy parent-child relationship, parents are also responsible for encouragement and challenge, setting clear rules and boundaries, and lovingly administering correction and discipline. Note: Respect and trust are earned; they cannot be demanded.

It is the same for our relationship with Jesus Christ. When we understand how much He loves us and trust that His rules are for our good and protection, we *want* to obey His commandments. We don't always do so, but our heart attitude becomes one of submission in gratitude for all He has done, rather than one of obeying out of duty. In the same way, children and adolescents who love and respect their parents will be more inclined to obey their directives because they know that their parents want what's best for them.

How does this play out in the area of sexuality? Building intimate relationships with one's children has been shown to contribute to their healthy sexual development. On the flipside, studies of teens who are sexually active report that 58 percent feel they never got to know their dad; 40 percent feel they never got to know their mom.[20]

Shame/Embarrassment

Some parents aren't talking because they feel a sense of embarrassment, even shame, concerning the human body and topics of sex. God created us male and female and saw that His creation was very good (Gen. 1:31); "And the man and his wife were both naked and were not ashamed" (Gen. 2:25). One bite of forbidden fruit and they found themselves ashamed of their nakedness and hiding from God (Gen. 3:7,10). What happened?

God, in His mercy, clothed them, but He did not eliminate their shame. Ever since, shame has manifested itself when we rebel against God's law. Just as with Adam and Eve, we want to hide our rebellious deeds from others, from God, and even from ourselves. And ever since Adam and Eve's rebellion, humanity has been naturally uncomfortable with nakedness.

*"And then my folks got all awkward and told me
that a human dropped me on their doorstep"*

This shame about nakedness then leaks into feelings of shame in talking about sex and sexuality.

All of humanity has this inborn sense of shame which can be constructive, destructive, or eradicated.

Constructive Shame

Shame can protect us by acting as a policeman or as speed bumps causing us to slow down. Ravi Zacharius has this to say about shame:

"Shame is to the moral health of a society what pain is to the body. Neither is pleasant, but both serve as warnings that our health is in danger."[21]

When we respond to shame and stop thinking or doing what is causing that shame, it serves a constructive, protective purpose.

The Eradication of Shame

Shame can also become unproductive and even destructive— destructive because parents are not arming their children with the moral and ethical filter they need as they go forth into the world.

One student said just this when asked why his parents wouldn't talk with him about sex: "Sex is a topic...they perceive as shameful. They believe that your body is something to be ashamed of."

This shame is manifested in two ways: first, in our use of euphemisms for body parts and functions associated with reproduction; second, in our embarrassment when questioned by our children about sex. Shame can be destructive when parents won't talk with their children about sex. Sex, discussed in a dignified manner, is not shameful.

By not talking, and by acting embarrassed by their children's sexual questions, parents impose their false sense of shame onto their children. False shame serves no constructive purpose. Children, in turn, are embarrassed and feel shamed when the topic of sex is broached, especially in a public setting such as school. However, as they grow up, they hear more and more sex talk, particularly from peers and the media. Through this constant barrage, their embarrassment and false sense of shame begin to wear away. With the assault upon this false shame, all shame wears thin—even shame, as Dr. Zacharius said above, which is ultimately vital to their moral health. When this happens, there is danger of the eradication of all shame. By the time adolescents are of dating age, having heard little to no teaching from their parents about how they are to handle their sexuality, they tend to follow the cultural leading of peers, media, and sometimes school, embarking on a period of sexual experimentation.

While parents often avoid talking about subjects they find embarrassing, they should remind themselves that God's design of the human body and plan for sexuality within marriage are beautiful and not inherently shameful. Discuss these things openly and in age-appropriate ways, beginning when your child is young and not easily embarrassed. You will become more confident and your child will learn that they can safely discuss this subject at home.

Fear of Our Own Histories

Finally, parents aren't talking because many of us fear "the question" from our children: "What about you, Mom/Dad. Were you virgins when you married?" It is very likely that well-talked-to children, particularly girls, will eventually ask this question or questions about Mom's/Dad's earlier dating life, and parents need to have thought about their answers before the questions come. This will be further discussed in Chapter 17: Telling the Truth.

Chapter 3

DOES TALKING HELP?

Parents aren't talking and their silence is a problem given today's world. What evidence, if any, indicates that parental conversation makes a difference? In other words, does talking help?

Evidence That Talking Helps

Research shows that talking helps to defuse the curiosity and certainly the sexual experimentation of youth. A 1998 study published by The Institute for Youth Development stated: "Clearly sexual promiscuity and high risk behavior can be reduced significantly if parents talk to their children about sex." The study goes on to say that 88% of high school students whose parents strongly urged them to be sexually abstinent were so. Whereas more than half (52%) of students that said their parents didn't care if they had sex, had engaged in sex.[22] An article in the *Journal of Adolescent Research* concurs: "Students who talked with their parents were less apt to be sexually experienced."[23]

Talking brings parents and children emotionally closer together. Anne Nesbit, a curriculum writer, affirms this: "It is imperative that strong bonds of communication be developed between parent and child in the area of sexuality.... Once communication in a sensitive area has been established between parents and children, it will continue during the adolescent years when the need for security becomes so essential."[24] In the preface to her book *My Body Book for Girls*, Lynda Madaras comments: "It's been my experience that kids are enormously grateful for the reassurance they get from such [sex] education.... Not only are kids grateful when their needs for reassurance are met in this way, but they also develop a profound respect for and trust in the source of that reassurance."[25]

Kids Listen

A study in the *Journal of the American Medical Association* (JAMA) concluded:

Adults have a powerful effect on their children's behavior right through the high school years.... The researchers found that if parents expected adolescents to get good grades and refrain from sex, those expectations influence the adolescents' behavior powerfully through 12th grade.... Adolescents are often very effective at convincing us that what we say is irrelevant to their lives, and the mistake we make as adults is that we turn around and we believe it.[26]

A study from The National Campaign to Prevent Teenage Pregnancy concurs: "In public opinion polling and other research, teens consistently say that parents influence their decisions about sex—more than peers, teachers, religious leaders, or the media...yet parents incorrectly believe that these other sources overshadow them.... They need to be reminded that is not the case."[27]

Adolescents are often very effective at convincing us that what we say is irrelevant to their lives; the problem is—we believe them.

Joshua and Beverly were engaged to be married and discussed, one day, how much talk about sex, love, dating and marriage had occurred in their families as they grew up. Joshua said that it was practically dinner table conversation in his family: constant and persistent. Beverly said her family never talked about any of those subjects. After this conversation Joshua called his mom and said,

"Do you remember all those conversations we had about sex, dating and stuff? The ones through which I mainly rolled my eyes?"

"Yes, I well remember," his mom replied. Then Joshua said words that were written indelibly on his mom's heart:

"Thanks, Mom!"

This is not unusual. Well-talked-to, grown children will often find occasion to thank their parents for guiding them, holding them to loving boundaries, and not allowing the subject of sex to be intimidating. Talking early and often gives needed information, grows strong relationships and models healthy conversational habits to guide our children when they raise their own families.

Walk a Little Slower Daddy

"Walk a little slower, Daddy," said a child so small.

"I'm following in your footsteps and I don't want to fall.

Sometimes your steps are very fast,

Sometimes they're hard to see;

So walk a little slower, Daddy, for you are leading me.

Someday when I'm all grown up,

You're what I want to be;

Then I will have a little child who'll want to follow me.

And I would want to lead just right, and know that I was true;

So walk a little slower, Daddy,

For I must follow you."

(Author Unknown)

A parent might say: "I understand that talking is important, but what happens if parents don't talk?" If parents don't talk to their young children about sex, the inquiry of their children is shut down. They stop asking their parents sexual questions. They take on adult embarrassment about this subject in polite company. On the other hand, around their peers they often begin to indulge in crude talk, thus making the subject of sex all about lust and desire and never about relationship and beauty.

Silence of Adolescence

Silence on the subject of sex can drive children away from their parents during the adolescent years. This may be a temporary situation or it may become permanent. A critical time exists when this subject needs to be initially addressed in families. If this doesn't happen by the time children move toward puberty, they often become private, defensive, and even hostile toward parental attempts to inquire about their social interests. Put rather bluntly, kids think: "You were too busy, too embarrassed, too hung up to talk with me about sex and bodies and what to expect as my body began to change, and *now* you want to know what I'm doing, if I'm interested in the opposite sex? Now you're trying to push your moral rules and sexual do's and don'ts, but you're too late!" They now feel their sexuality is none of your business. They're not going to listen to you.

They Act Out Their Curiosity

Un-talked-to children act out their curiosity and too often indulge in sexual experimentation. The Center of Disease Control (CDC) cumulative chart on the following page breaks down the age of first sexual intercourse according to data in 1995.

Of course, with sexual intercourse comes the possibility of pregnancy. In 2009 the CDC data states that although teen birth rates are down, "they remain higher than those in most industrialized nations."[28]

Remember, birth rates and pregnancy rates are two different things: Pregnancy rates are all women who become pregnant but not all pregnancies end in the birth of a baby. Birth rates are all pregnancies minus miscarriages and abortions.

Age of First Sexual Intercourse

Age	Males	Females
13	3.9%	3%
14	11%	8%
15	21.3%	18.6%
16	35.2%	31.9%
17	52.6%	47.4%
18	65.1%	59.2%
19	83.4%	69.7%

CDC 1995 cumulative chart of those who have had sexual intercourse.[29]

Sexually Transmitted Diseases (STD's)

Enormous amounts of statistics exist about sexually transmitted diseases. Along with a few more statistics (below), suffice it to say these diseases have caused a crisis in adolescent health.

➤ Genital herpes is reported to have infected 20% of people in the U.S. age 12 and older.[30]

➤ [P]retty much everyone who's sexually active (multiple sexual partners) is going to get HPV.[31] HPV (Human Papilomavirus) can cause genital warts which can develop into various cancers of the reproductive organs.

➤ Approximately one in four sexually active teens contract a sexually transmitted disease (STD) yearly.[32]

➤ More than 4,000 teens contract a sexually transmitted disease *daily*.[33]

> In 2007, statistics indicated around 1.1 million Americans were living with Human Immunodeficiency Virus (HIV, the AIDS virus).[34]

No risk is present for the ones who save sex for marriage and remain monogamous in their marriages.

Abortion

Frederica Matthews Green has stated: "No woman wants an abortion as she wants an ice cream cone or a Porsche. She wants an abortion as an animal caught in a trap wants to gnaw off its leg."[35]

Once the moral consensus "sex is for marriage" reversed and sex outside of marriage became quite common, many women found themselves pregnant and feeling trapped: not married, not ready for a baby, too young, scared, poor, alone, etc. Women are often told that abortion is no big deal—just tissue which will be scraped out of their uterus. Abortion, at the time, may seem like the only way out, but over time it proves to be exceedingly painful for most women. Many, particularly young women, feel devastated, hopeless and worthless. They do not feel as if they can talk about their feelings and so carry a heavy burden of shame and pain.

Abortion has affected one in five women in the Evangelical Protestant church and one in three in the Catholic church.[36]

Children Turn Elsewhere for Information

Children come early to understand that talking about sex is not something their parents are comfortable doing. They have observed their parents pointing their questions to someone else—"Ask your father/teacher/friend/pastor!"—or they have been told that they are too young to know the answer. What better way to fuel the fire of curiosity than to tell children they are too young to know about something they have asked about? Because their parents have made it clear, either verbally or non-verbally, that they do not want to talk about sex, children stop asking. Children are then faced with the question, "What do I do with all my unanswered questions and burning curiosity?" What they do is turn to other sources for information.

Someone's Talking. Who Is It?

Where do kids turn with their unanswered questions about sex? Is it to Dad? the Church? Media? Mom? Peers? School? Take a moment and rank these sources according to who you think kids turn to first, then see the following chart.

Where Kids Get Information About Sex

Peers	49 %
Media	28 %
Mom	12 %
School	7 %
Dad	3 %
Church	1 %

Dennis Rainey[37]

The Implications

If nearly half the information about sex comes from peers, where do peers get their information? What is the ethical content, if any, in the information? Is the information even accurate?

A friend's daughter overheard the following conversation on a school bus:

"What are condoms used for?"

"Condoms are used by men so that they don't go to the bathroom while having sex."

If only seven percent of a child's information about sex comes from teaching at school, a whole lot of money is being spent with little to show for it. And how much ethical content can be expected from that public school teaching?

I think a good part of the reason why little information is retained from what is taught at school is because the topic is taught early and many of the students are so embarrassed by the content that they do not hear what is being taught. This is especially true for students who have not talked at home. Here's what I mean. I taught health education in a middle school for five years. In the fifth grade, students were to learn about their bodies: reproductive parts were named and functions were reviewed. The administration was adamant about this being done in integrated classes (boys and girls together). Not many years ago this subject matter was delayed until high school and then taught in sex-separate classes. Now many school administrations state that they want sex education to be just like any other subject. But it is far from any other subject in the minds of many students who view the subject as highly embarrassing and shameful.

(Many of them have *never* heard these terms used before, and certainly not in public.) I will never forget the response of many young girls who were virulently embarrassed with this public discussion of reproduction and body parts. The subject, for many, had been shrouded in mystery and darkness—never mentioned in their families. Now, suddenly, the subject is on public display in a sexually mixed classroom. This is not an ideal venue for learning to take place!

It's obvious that very few churches are dealing with the topic of sex. The combined percentage for mom, dad, and church is only 16%; yet home and church are where the ethical content of sex education needs to be taught. Because the church is doing such an abysmal job of talking about sex and God's intent for its use, more and more Christian young people are growing up not knowing that God intended sex only for marriage as part of the deeply intimate relationship between a husband and wife.

An article in a Christian college newspaper highlights this:

> There are many students from conservative or Christian educational backgrounds that are misinformed or unaware about sex and all it entails.
>
> 'Ignorance is bliss' for many college students until they realize the cost of acting with little knowledge for what could potentially become a life changing situation for parent and child....[38]

No one has ever told them about cause and effect and why sex is to be saved for marriage. Much room for improvement exists here.

It is not a question of preventing children from getting information, it is a question of who is going to lead them.

Communication Through Developmental Stages

Chapter 4

THE FIRST CONVERSATIONS

The first conversations should begin as soon as children understand language. In these early, simple conversations at least two things are happening: you are providing the vocabulary for future talks and you begin the process of building a close, trusting relationship. Sex is one of the hardest topics to talk about, but starting early gives parents time to become comfortable and adept in talking about this topic. Furthermore, consider this: *If you can talk about sex, you can talk about anything.*

Owning Our Feelings

Before you begin, you need to inventory your own feelings. If this topic is embarrassing to you, admit it. Pray for God to show you the beauty of His whole creation, including the human body. Ask for confidence in conversing with your children. Practice with your spouse or a good friend. Even if your first conversations happen when your children are older, talk! Open with something like:

"You may find this embarrassing. I feel the same way, but it is something we need to talk about."

Or: "I know this is embarrassing, but remember, I've been an adolescent too."

Whether your child is young or older, you don't need to be an expert on sex. When things come up that you are not sure about, tell them you will try to find out. Let your children know that when they want information, or just want to talk, you are the best place to start.

Naming Body Parts and Functions Correctly

One of the first steps is the naming of body parts and functions. As you name the major body parts (eyes, ears, nose, mouth, arms, legs) continue to name their genitals: penis or vagina.

Communication is difficult, if not impossible, if we won't use correct names for things. Think how hard it would be to get someone's attention if you didn't know their name.

Dottie was pregnant and had just had her first ultrasound when her grandmother came to visit.

"Did you see the dingus?" asked her grandmother

"Dingus"? thought Dottie. "I wonder what that is?" She asked her grandmother for further explanation. Her grandmother, greatly embarrassed and searching for words, finally said,

"You know, the part between the legs. Is it a boy or a girl?"

Vicki Courtney tells how she had provided her children with nicknames for body parts.

My little nickname system worked just fine until one day when a new family moved into our neighborhood. I had heard that they also had a six-year-old boy, the same age as my oldest at the time, so we stopped by one day to introduce ourselves. When the mother introduced her son to my son, Ryan, I immediately knew we had a problem. Unfortunately, he shared the same name as um, well, you know—I still can't say it! Anyway, I shot my son a pleading look to remain silent, but by the look on his face, I knew we would have plenty to talk about on the way home. I'll never forget his comment as we walked away: "Mom, why would anyone name their kid Willy?"[39]

Being open about body part names and functions can, instead, allow for fun conversations with our children.

Early simple talking opens the topic, gives vocabulary and builds relationship.

Sue was driving her adolescent boys to do some shopping during a school holiday. As they drove by Dick's Sporting Goods, her teens in the back of the van started giggling.

"What are you giggling about?" she asked.

"Last week," they told her, "when we were driving by here with Joe, his father said, 'Wow, what a big Dick's.'" (They chose only to hear "Dick.")

Sue joined in the giggles and they enjoyed a playful moment. The boys then started a discussion about the strange names people use for reproductive parts. Sue agreed that indeed people do think up strange names. Then they asked,

"Did your family use funny names when you were growing up?" "Yup," she replied. She told them the ones she remembered but said she had forgotten some of them. Finally, her 14-year-old son asked,

"Why can't people just call it a penis?"

"Exactly!" said Sue. "Why can't they?"

When naming body parts and functions, think about whether the names you offer reflect the wonder of the way we are created, "fearfully and wonderfully made" as Psalm 139:14 tells us.

Correct Misunderstandings

Kids say the darndest things! Nevertheless, after you enjoy their interpretation don't let the opportunity to correct misunderstandings pass.

A three-year-old went with his father to look at a litter of kittens. Breathlessly, he came back to his mother and said:

"We saw three boy kittens and two girl kittens."

"How do you know?" asked his mom.

"Oh, daddy turned them over. I think it was stamped on the bottom."[40]

Give them a hug, enjoy their enthusiasm, then simply say, "No, it's not stamped on the bottom. Daddy was looking to see if the kittens had a penis or a vagina. Boys have penises and girls have vaginas."

Johnny, having just seen the boys' puberty movie in school, was telling his father what he had learned. He was describing "wet dreams" when he said something about his "weeness."

"Do you mean penis?" asked his father.

"Oh, yes, penis."

The conversation continued with the father making sure the son had the correct information.

Steve, in middle school, was with his mom and a friend doing some errands. Suddenly, Steve asked,

"Mom, what are rubbers?"

"Rubbers are covers you put on your feet when it's raining so that your shoes don't get wet."

"Oh," replied Steve, seemingly satisfied.

It was a beautiful, cloudless day and Steve's mom began to wonder where this question had come from.

"What made you ask that?" She continued.

"Oh, a bus just went by and it had a big sign on it which said, "Don't forget your rubbers."

His mom had also seen the bus and remembered the sign. Time to correct a misunderstanding!

"Oh, well actually, that sign wasn't referring to rubbers that keep your feet dry. That sign was talking about condoms. 'Don't forget your condoms.'"

"What are condoms?" asked Steve.

"Condoms are like a sock that a man puts on his penis to collect sperm if he is having sexual intercourse and wants to decrease the likelihood of his wife getting pregnant."

In the course of a conversation like this you may find it appropriate to add something about how sex is a good gift from God to be used when married. If your child wants more specific information he'll ask either then or later when his friend isn't present.

Jack arrived home from school to find a package that had come in the mail. He brought it inside and said to his mother,

"I thought that stuff was illegal to send though the mail!"

"Read it more carefully," said his mom. "It doesn't say 'pornographic records,' it says 'phonograph records.'"

She had received materials packed in an old box. But Jack's next question caused her to feel as old as the box:

"What are phonograph records?"

How Much Is Too Much?

Taking about sex with our children begs the question "How much information is too much?" In her book *How You Are Changing* Jane Graver offers the following note to parents: "Too much information does not seem to do any harm when linked to positive values. The child who feels unable to ask questions is far more apt to become preoccupied with sex than the one who has open access to information."[41] If too much is given too soon, they won't hear what they're not interested in.

A mom was getting five-year-old David and three-year-old Katie ready for bed. They were naked when her son asked,

"Why doesn't Katie have a penis?"

During the ensuing conversation between mom and son, Katie was dancing around the room paying little attention, although she did hear the final comment from her mother,

"So boys have a penis and girls have a vagina."

The dancing three-year-old Katie began to sing "and vaginas come from China."

The conversation didn't interest her and she wasn't listening. But she knew she could ask and she would remember that there was no embarrassment or awkwardness, just casual conversation.

Philip had heard about puberty changes in girls and boys both from his mother and at school. He had been taught that girls/women get their "period" every month once they became mature women. One day, after he was engaged to be married, he came home, aghast, and said,

"I didn't know that when women get their periods they bleed for four to five days!"

"Well, what did you think happened?" asked his mom.

"I thought it was similar to urinating. You went to the toilet and 'had your period.' It was done just like that."

"Where were you when we talked about women and menstruation?" replied his mom with an affectionate laugh.

His next comment endeared him even more to his mother: "Wow, women really have it rough!"

The point is, that young man had had several sessions of teaching about the puberty changes of girls, but it didn't affect him and he didn't listen. It went right over his head.

If answers and explanations are given by a trusted, loving source (parents), you don't need to worry about what is too much.

43

Keeping the Topic Open

One major way to keep the topic open is to recognize and unpack teachable moments. A teachable moment is easily recognized when your kids ask questions. These questions will often come while watching TV or noticing the messages in magazine advertisements or billboards along the highway. If your child asks about, or even tries out, dirty words or gestures, don't overreact but explain what those words/gestures really mean and discourage their use. Point out how demeaning these can be.

You can actually orchestrate teachable moments by reading age-appropriate books together. Look for an age-graded book on sex and sexual development. Read it to or with them, then talk about what you read or just be available for their questions or wonderment. Don't just give them the book to read by themselves. Read it to or with them.[42]

Once you recognize teachable moments, think about ways to unpack them. As your children get older and issues arise, after talking with them about the issue, look for books or biblical stories that will further flesh out the issue. Using other people's stories helps illustrate the pain and sometimes shame caused when we act in wrong ways, but does so without focusing repeatedly on your child's behavior. For example, when talking about marital fidelity, read or point out stories in the media of someone caught in an adulterous affair and the fallout for all involved.

Answer All Questions with Correct Answers

Questions should be answered accurately and appropriately—not necessarily with all you know, but with enough detail to satisfy.

In a bathroom stall at an airport, the following conversation ensued between a mother and her young son:

"What's that?"

"That's the place where women throw their used tampons."

"What are tampons?"

"Tampons are used to absorb the blood that happens when women get their periods."

"What's a period?"

"Periods happen once a month unless a woman is pregnant. It is the way a woman's body has of cleaning itself."

Apparently satisfied, mom and son continued on their way. That was a lot of information for a young boy to absorb. No doubt, he'll repeat his questions again and again until he's old enough to understand.

If you don't know the answer, assure your children that you will find out. Do your research, then get back to them in a timely fashion.

Answer questions but add the venue discussion—where it is appropriate to talk about these things. Young children are quite observant, but live in the present. If the place where they ask their question is not appropriate for discussion, tell them so, but assure them that you will get back to it when you return home. By the time you get home they may have forgotten their question, but bring it up with them: "You asked me about _____ when we were _____." Then give them the answer. Take, for example, the child who asks, usually in a loud voice, "Why is that lady so fat?"

"She's not fat, she's going to have a baby."

"How did the baby get inside her?"

Remind them that sex and reproduction are topics to discuss in the privacy of their home. These are not discussions they should have with their young peers. It's like the Santa Claus issue. If parents have chosen to inform their kids that Santa Claus is a lot of fun but he's a myth, each family's approach should be respected.

Don't forget to ask clarifying questions. Consider the child who asked his mother, "Mom, where did I come from?" Mom, thinking he was asking about how he was born, carefully explained about her pregnancy and his birth. At the end of her talk he said, "No, I mean did I come from New York or California?"

With your older children (seventh grade and older), ask questions of them that will tell you what they've learned. You might ask: "What have you heard us tell you about sex...alcohol...dating?" Question their understanding of the subject matter in books or movies asking: "What conclusions can be drawn from that story?" Do not miss the rich opportunities to talk to them about advertisements. Help them to understand the real message behind ads, pointing out the subtle messages presented. Don't be afraid to use negative messages in order to help them understand what healthy sexuality is. Ads are often fast-paced and the subtleties are easy to miss. If you have the ability to record TV advertisements, do so, then encourage your kids to study the ads. Make a game of it! One father offered a monetary reward if his kids could pinpoint what was really being said.

If you can talk about sex, you can talk about anything.

Chapter 5

THE EARLY YEARS

We've looked at why and how to have ongoing dialogue about sexuality with our children, beginning when they're young. But which topics should be discussed when?

Preschool and Early Grades

In the preschool years it is natural to discuss body parts. Make short, factual statements to teach or to answer questions. You may need to start these conversations; don't wait for them to ask. This may become increasingly true as they get older.

Be prepared to answer questions about boy/girl differences. Talk about where babies come from. If your child doesn't ask, find ways to initiate these discussions. Look for an age-graded book to read to them about reproduction.[43]

Use Analogies

A pregnant mother and her four-year-old son were in the flower garden planting in the spring.

"Mommy, how did the baby get inside your tummy?"

"Daddies and mommies have a special way of hugging and sometimes a baby starts to grow."

"But how did the baby get inside your tummy?"

He was quite insistent on knowing more, so she went on, using the analogy of planting seeds:

"My finger is like daddy's penis. This seed is like the seeds that daddies have in their bodies. Mommies have tiny eggs in their bodies. When daddies and mommies hug each other in a special way, daddy puts his penis into mommy's vagina. Mommy's vagina is like this hole where the seed goes. When daddy's penis is in mommy's vagina, the seed from daddy sometimes connects with an egg inside mommy's body and a baby starts to grow."

Point out animals or birds in their mating behaviors. These are fascinating to watch.

We had a bird box right outside of our dining room window. For many years, bluebirds took up residency in that box. We greatly enjoyed watching the cycle of life. One day we had a family join us for lunch. It was spring and the birds were all about mating. At one point in our after-dinner conversation, someone pointed out the mating birds. The mother turned around to look, quickly turning back with an obvious shudder of embarrassment.

This is nothing to be embarrassed by; use such things as teaching tools.

Prepare Them for Puberty

With puberty starting earlier and earlier, children need to be prepared for the changes that will take place in their bodies. Ideally, they should understand about their anticipated body changes two years before changes begin to occur. This gives them lots of time to prepare for what is going to happen and to process their feelings about these changes. See the following charts for physical changes and anticipated timing of these changes in puberty. On these charts are the usual order and timing of change. As with everything to do with human growth, exceptions occur, but this will give you some idea of what to expect. The onset of puberty is often related to the age that mom and dad started puberty. Of course, this is only helpful if both parents were early, in between, or late. If one parent started early and the other late, then it's anyone's guess as to when their children will start puberty.

Physical Changes in Puberty

GIRLS

Range	Average	Duration of changes
8-15	10-12	4 years

Order of changes:

Height, Weight, Breasts, Vaginal Discharge, Menstrual Periods

Chart: Girls

Notice that usually girls start into puberty one to three years before boys. Their first change is a growth spurt. Typically, girls stop growing around ages 15-16.

Weight Gain

Girls need to be reminded that with an increase in height comes an associated increase in weight. Weight can be a huge issue for young women, so this is a key time to initiate ongoing conversations about body image, appropriate weight, and proper nutrition.

Breast and Hair Development

When breasts start to develop it is common for them to develop at different rates. For awhile, one breast might look bigger than the other. Assure your daughters that this is only temporary and that breast growth will even out in time. The first pubic hairs will be seen around this time.

Vaginal Discharge and Menstrual Periods

Vaginal discharge may occur up to two years before a girl's first menstrual period. It should be clear, of egg white consistency. It should have no odor and it should not be accompanied by itching. If it is green or yellowish, if it has an odor, or if there is itching, be alert for a possible infection. Some girls are sensitive to certain hygiene products.

The first menstrual period usually occurs when a girl's weight approaches 90-100 pounds. A certain amount of body fat is needed before the body will prepare for the possibility of pregnancy. Fat is a great insulator against heat loss and the body is designed to provide this protection for a possible resident in the womb. Women athletes with little body fat will often skip many menstrual periods, if not stop menstruating completely, until their body fat increases.

Ova or Eggs

Girls are born with about 250,000 (a quarter million!) immature ova. At puberty, as part of the monthly menstrual cycle, these begin to ripen, usually one at a time. A woman only uses about 800-900 ova in a lifetime. Take time to wonder with your daughter about how we are "fearfully and wonderfully made" (Psalm 139:14). Ova stop ripening at menopause, usually between the ages of 40 and 50, when the remaining ova are absorbed by the body.

Physical Changes in Puberty

BOYS

Range	Average	Duration of changes
8-16	11-13	4 years

Order of changes:

Scrotum, Penis, Ejaculation, Height, Weight, Hair, Voice

Chart: Boys

Usually the physical changes at puberty in boys begin where no one can see—with an enlarging scrotum and a penis that gets longer, bigger, and darker in color.

Nocturnal Emissions

Sometime after this, a boy can expect that he might begin to have occasional nocturnal emissions ("wet dreams"). This is a nighttime ejaculation of sperm and semen. Some feel that this is the way the body deals with overproduction of sperm. It is about 1-2 teaspoons of thick, sticky, jelly-like liquid. But if a pubescent male does not expect the possibility of such an emission, he might think that he has wet his bed. For some boys, the end of nighttime bedwetting might not be very far distant from occasional nighttime emissions. Not all boys/men experience these emissions, which may or may not be connected with a dream. Again, reassurance is helpful to let your son know that if he experiences these, they are perfectly normal and nothing to be concerned about. Such emissions alert him to the fact that he now has an adult male body.

Growth Spurt

After these hidden changes, boys begin to increase in height and weight. This can be rather dramatic (and expensive) over a period of a couple of years. During this time you have to keep buying new clothes because they outgrow the others so quickly. Typically, boys begin their growth spurt around age 12-13, with rapid growth for at least a year; but they may continue to grow until about age 19. Because a boy's growth spurt is later than a girl's, girls are taller than boys throughout much of middle school. By high school, boys are generally taller than girls.

Body Hair and Voice Changes

During this time your sons will notice growth of body hair and, near the end of these changes, their voice will begin to change, getting lower and sounding more like dad's.

Breast Changes

It is very important to alert your sons to the possibility of some breast change. Fifty to eighty-five percent of boys will have some breast change at the beginning of puberty. Often a boy might notice a small nubbin under his nipple (on one or both sides). This can happen as a result of hormone levels shifting but is nothing to be concerned about. If this happens, it will resolve itself without treatment when hormone levels settle down, usually within 12-18 months.[44] Nevertheless, it can be embarrassing to boys and may cause some distress, particularly if they have to dress and undress in open locker rooms or when swimming. Give them lots of reassurance and suggestions as to how to limit their embarrassment. When they want to swim, for example, you might suggest they wear a dark t-shirt or swim shirt. Talk to them about options for locker room privacy.

Sperm

Boys are not born with sperm. Sperm start to develop at puberty and continue to develop throughout a male's lifetime. Approximately 40 million sperm are released in a single ejaculation. Once again, marvel with your sons at how we are "fearfully and wonderfully made" (Psalm 139:14). And talking about being "fearfully and wonderfully made," when talking to them about their physical development, explain to them that within each testicle is the vas deferens, a microscopic tube. This tube is coiled around and around and packed into the space of the thimble-size testicle. If it were to be stretched out, it would stretch the length of a football field!

Discuss School/Peer Issues

Talk about issues that come up in school or with other children. Mentioned earlier was an article on MSNBC reporting an inappropriate recess game in a Minnesota elementary school called "rape tag."[45] This is an extreme example but a good illustration. What's a parent to do? As soon as a parent hears about an inappropriate situation, go to the principal or other school authority. Find out exactly what the situation is, then begin a conversation. Find out what your child knows or has heard. Correct any misunderstandings or exaggerations they may have heard. If they haven't heard, inform them in a general way to prepare them for any talk among their peers. In this case, the "rape" part of the game was a simulation of sex or "humping." Once a person was tagged, they were "frozen" until released by the simulated act. Talk about what's wrong with such a game and ask them what they should do if faced with such a situation. Emphasize that if they become aware of any such inappropriate behavior, they should go immediately to a teacher and report it. Ask, at the end of the conversation, if they have any questions. If they do, answer those. If not, encourage them to come back to you with anything further that comes up. Check in with them later by asking about what they are hearing at school, and ask again if they have any other questions.

If they ask outright what rape means, give them a simple explanation such as: "sexual intercourse happening to someone who does not want it." Make sure they know how to keep themselves safe (not to let anyone touch or ask to see their private parts; get away from the situation; inform a trusted adult immediately).

Once a question is asked, if it is not answered by a parent, kids will look elsewhere to find the answer. As stated before, if kids are told they are too young to know (or some similar message) it only increases their curiosity. And what will they hear or read when they turn to the Internet or peers? It's not a matter of preventing them from getting their questions answered. The issue is: Who is going to answer their questions? Who is going to educate them? The idea here is to give them a minimal amount of information and then let them lead the conversation. Allow and encourage them to ask questions that you answer. They do not need graphic information, just a truthful answer to their questions. In this you do three things: you satisfy their curiosity (you may defuse a possible hot issue); you make it clear that they can come to you to ask for information; and you demonstrate that you want to be the one talking to them about these subjects.

Bullying

Bullying is a terrible scourge, greatly exacerbated by Facebook, Myspace, and other social media. While children are in elementary school, bullying usually occurs on the playground through unkind comments or "teasing," which can often be defused at home.

John came home from third grade terribly upset. When his mom asked the cause of his pain, he described the playground scene where there was a lot of unkind teasing going on. He felt humiliated. John spent a good deal of time crying and unloading onto his mom. Even though trying to stay calm, his mom was enraged. "How could anyone treat my son this way?" She asked herself.

Aloud, she said: "Do you want some help with this?"

"No," he answered, now dry eyed, and went outside and played happily the rest of the afternoon.

The lesson learned by that mom was that at least some of the wounding from cruel peers can be undone by a kind, listening ear. Once kids have "gotten it off their chest" and know they have a safe haven at home, they seem better able to cope.

As they get toward the age when many of their friends will be using social media, you will need to revisit this issue of bullying. Explain to them what bullying is, if they don't know. Ask your children if they have faced bullying of any kind. If they have, help them develop strategies to cope. Ask: "Is what they are saying about you true?" If the answer is no, then encourage your child to do his best to ignore what's said but come home and talk about it. If the answer is yes, work with him to change his behavior. Encourage him to stay away from the people who are being cruel. Do your best to build your child up, letting him know how much you love him. Point out the things he does well and encourage him to invite friends home. He needs to know he has an ally.

Father/Son or Mother/Daughter Weekend

This is a good time to consider a father/son or mother/daughter weekend away to talk more intensively about the things your children will face as they enter adolescence: puberty changes, purity, feelings, and emotions. Look for good resources for such a retreat, for example Passport2Purity from Dennis and Barbara Rainey's FamilyLife ministry.[46]

Chapter 6

MIDDLE SCHOOL

The following major topics should be discussed with your child during the middle school years (between ages 12 and 15): reproduction, masturbation, homosexuality, STD's, social media, and pornography (discussed in Chapter 7).

Reproduction

By the age of 12, your children should have a thorough understanding of the whole reproduction cycle. Both sexes should know about menstruation, the cycle, and the reason for menstruation. Daughters need to know how to deal with their periods so they will be prepared when the time comes. Both sexes should understand about male puberty: What are nocturnal emissions? Why do they happen? Do all boys have "wet dreams"?

By middle school age, children should understand what sexual intercourse is and how one gets pregnant. This is an ideal age to take them through the amazing process of fetal development. Watch a DVD about the beginning of life, like Nova's "The Miracle of Life"[47] which shows with beautiful photography a life from conception to birth.

Another way to engage them in the wonder of being is to ask: "Have you ever won a race?" If they answer yes, then ask: "But have you ever won a race against 40 million others?"

No doubt they will say no.

"You are wrong!" you can tell them. "You won your very first race. It was you against 40 million others, *and you won!*" Explain that of those 40 million or more sperm that are released with an ejaculation and are racing to find an ova (egg), only one will win and fertilize the egg. "You won your first race! *You* were meant to be!"

Along with the menstrual cycle, explain fertility, birth control, and contraception. Explain the difference between a contraceptive and birth control: a contraceptive is anything that prevents the sperm and egg coming together; birth control is anything which prevents birth. Abortion, for example, is a form of birth control. This information is not for their use now, but so they will understand what their peers or teachers are talking about.

Masturbation

Masturbation is a subject often avoided within families. It's a hard subject to tackle even with your spouse, given its many attached myths and charged information. But it's something our children want and need us as parents to address. To try to talk about masturbation cold, without having built relationship and trust, is probably not going to happen. But for parents who have talked with their children about sex and sexuality all along, this subject is just another one of many informational sessions for preadolescents.

One way to approach the subject is to read with them from one of the age-graded books about sexual development. In the book *Sex and the New You*, Richard Bimler puts it this way: "A Majority of both boys and girls masturbate at some time in their lives. Masturbation is the handling or rubbing of the penis or clitoris to gain pleasure or until release of sexual pressure, or orgasm, is reached."[48]

If you choose to introduce the topic through a book, read it together and talk about it after. Make sure they understand all the words used. The clitoris, for example, is a bundle of nerves about the size of a pea located at the top of a woman's vulva, above the urethral opening. It is very sensitive and is responsible for feelings of sexual pleasure when stimulated. An orgasm is a series of pleasurable muscular contractions experienced at the peak of sexual excitement, usually resulting from stimulation of the sexual organ. In males it is usually accompanied by ejaculation of sperm.

A good follow-up question after reading about masturbation might be: "Is this something you've wondered about?" Let them lead the conversation from there. Check back with them after awhile, reminding them that masturbation is something you talked about: "Any thoughts on this subject?"

What you teach your children about this subject is up to you. If you are not sure how you feel about it, you need to wrestle with it. Talk it over with your spouse, trusted friends, your pastor, a counselor (if you know one). Read differing opinions on the subject, then decide how you are going to approach the subject with your children.

Note two things. First, the Bible is silent on this subject (but has a lot to say about lust). Second, committed Christians differ in their opinion about the subject: some say no one should masturbate ever, while others see it more as a pressure release when all else fails, to be indulged in with great caution.

Percentages of those who masturbate is a difficult figure to obtain. Surveys indicate that ninety percent or more of men masturbate at some time in their lives, while about fifty percent of women do. Of course, just because many do doesn't necessarily make it OK. Masturbation is a frequently-discussed topic among men on Christian college campuses. Given the anxiety surrounding this subject, it needs to be addressed.

Four Principles about Masturbation

Less is best, none is better. This principle doesn't put a hard and fast "never" on the behavior, but does suggest it is best that it be a rare occurrence.

Walk the difficult line between guilt and obsession. This is advice given by a psychologist. Those who hold to an absolute "never masturbate" tend to be concerned that even occasional masturbation will inevitably lead to obsession, whereas others are concerned that an absolute "don't do it" message will result in a huge burden of guilt for those who struggle and struggle and just are unable to avoid the behavior entirely.

A third important principle, for those who allow for infrequent masturbation: do not let masturbation become linked to pornography. If linked to pornography, one tends to have virtual relationships which interfere with real relationships. No one can compete with unrealistic models touched up and airbrushed to perfection.

Finally, do not allow masturbation to become a substitute in marriage.

Homosexuality

The subject of homosexuality may well have come up even before middle school. If children are attending public schools, some teaching content about homosexuality is apt to be mandated. Be aware of what is being taught in your children's classrooms and be prepared to discuss it with them. Consider some of what Scripture has to say, looking together at the following:

Genesis 1:27: God made us to be image bearers of Him. He made us male and female—His image is complete in male plus female.

God gives a definition of marriage in His Word right at the beginning: "Therefore a man shall leave his father and his mother and hold fast [be joined] to his wife, and they shall become one flesh" (Genesis 2:24).

The word for joined or hold fast is the same word for "glued" or "stuck to." Marriage is a union between one man and one woman, and sex is given to us as a good gift to be used solely within that marriage. God intended sex in marriage to integrate the two halves of the sexual spectrum: male and female.

Matthew 19:3-12: Jesus acknowledges that marriage is not for everyone but indicates that when marriage takes place it is to be between a man and a woman.

1 Corinthians 6:9-11 lists some of the things that, if indulged in without repentance, will keep people from the Kingdom of Heaven, homosexuality being one. But as with the other sins listed, with repentance, forgiveness is available.

In the book of Ephesians the Apostle Paul clearly draws a comparison between human marriage and Christ's love for His church (Ephesians 5:31-32).

Among other understandings which can be drawn from this passage, Paul contrasts differences. He talks about different entities being joined together: a male and a female (one of each sex) and Christ with His church (Creator and creature).

The Institute for American Values' updated report, which was signed by an impressive list of family scholars, gave an A+ rating to the intact, biological family: "The intact, biological, married family remains the gold standard for family life in the United States, insofar as children are most likely to thrive—economically, socially, and psychologically—in this family form."[49] Of course, the biological family would mean a man and a woman parenting their own offspring.

There is, as yet, no research reporting on the psychological, economic, and social health of children brought up in families headed by homosexual couples. This is such a new phenomenon that not enough time has elapsed between this family makeup and children growing into adulthood to draw any significant conclusions. On the other hand, we have at least 4,000 years of evidence that the "intact, married, biological family" is, in general, a healthy place for children to grow.

Remind your children that God designed sex solely for (heterosexual) marriage. So the person sleeping with a boyfriend or girlfriend outside of marriage is going against God's way just as much as a homosexual involved in sex with someone of the same sex.

Recent statistics from The National Center for Disease Control and Prevention reported only 1.4 percent of the U.S. population claims a same-sex orientation.[50] Martin Hallett, involved in a ministry to gay and lesbian people (True Freedom Trust), states: "There are probably nearly as many

Christians with homosexual feelings who do not believe that homosexual sex is right for Christians as there are those who are advocating its acceptance."[51]

Young people also need to understand the difference between attraction and behavior. When the Bible talks about homosexuality, it is talking about sex between two men or two women. The Bible never speaks against a deeply caring, loving, even intimate (without sex) relationship between two people who happen to be of the same sex. David and Jonathan were very, very close friends. They shared an intimate, non-sexual love for each other: "As soon as he had finished speaking to Saul, the soul of Jonathan was knit to the soul of David and Jonathan loved him as his own soul" (1 Samuel 18:1). "And Saul spoke to Jonathan his son and to all his servants, that they should kill David. But Jonathan, Saul's son, delighted much in David" (1 Samuel 19:1).

Some people of the same sex choose to live together as roommates for their entire adult lives, sharing much in common but without sex. This is not what is termed in Scripture as homosexuality.

In his book *Washed and Waiting*, Wesley Hill very helpfully lays out the intense difficulty, indeed agony, of being a 'homosexual Christian': "For as long as I could remember, I had been drawn, even as a child, to other males in some vaguely confusing way, and after puberty, I had come to realize that I had a steady, strong, unremitting, exclusive sexual attraction to persons of the same sex."[52] He goes on to affirm that the position of the Christian church throughout the ages has remained the same: "...homosexuality was not God's original creative intention for humanity.... It is, on the contrary, a tragic sign of human nature and relationship being fractured by sin, and therefore...homosexual practice goes against God's express will for all human beings, especially those who trust in Christ."[53]

It is important that parents discuss with their children how they are to treat those who see this issue differently. We are called to love one another. We are called to be gentle and kind, not bashing others nor being ugly, nor being condemning. We are to gently speak God's truth but leave judgment to the Lord.

A pastor in a California community was invited to speak about homosexuality to a group of students on a college campus. The room was so packed with students that many were sitting on the floor leaving very little room to move. The pastor gave a winsome presentation addressing, among other things, the "hard things" the Bible has to say about sex and some of our behaviors. At one point he talked about how, in general, homosexuals struggle with a great deal of depression and have a much higher suicide rate. At the end of his talk, one student angrily challenged him saying that he was never depressed, he loved his life and he was an upbeat kind of person. Someone else in the room, a friend of the angry student, raised his hand and asked the first student: "If you are never depressed and love your life, why is it that you attempted to kill yourself last week?" Silence fell in the room and the pastor finished his time with the students. He made his way slowly through the tightly-packed crowd and, almost to a person, each one reached up to touch this man. He had presented ideas and explanations that some of those students disagreed with, but had done so in such a gentle and kind way that each one was deeply impacted.

Another pastor wrote several articles in a local newspaper while his state was debating civil unions and homosexual marriage. He received a response from a self-identified homosexual male who encouraged the pastor to continue to share his biblically-based views on homosexuality because, he said, "if you stop we will no longer have any hope."

Teach your children how to be kind and gentle when they disagree with others.

At times we may need to warn or remind our children about the physical boundaries they need to maintain with others.

Joe, a high school student, had an active interest in electronics. Jerry, an older man who lived down the street, had a similar interest. Jerry began to spend a good deal of time with Joe, often inviting him to his house. The problem was that these invitations usually came when Jerry's wife was not at home. Joe's parents talked about the situation and both agreed that they were concerned about the amount of time Joe was spending alone with Jerry at his home. They felt the need to talk to Joe about maintaining appropriate boundaries and planning what to do if something inappropriate began to happen. They agreed that the mom, who had the most one-on-one contact with Joe, should look for an opportunity to talk about the situation.

A short time later, Joe and his mom were driving to an appointment. At the beginning of the drive the mom brought up the subject and shared her concern, basically stating that it didn't seem to be a good idea for Joe to spend a lot of time alone with Jerry. The mom emphasized the fact that neither she nor Joe's dad had any reason to suspect ill intent from Jerry, but that they wanted to be certain Joe knew what to do if he began to feel uncomfortable.

Joe fell silent and said nothing for the rest of the trip. On the way home the awkward silence continued. Finally, just before arriving home, Joe began to talk. Nothing had happened, but he asked questions about his parents' concern and he and his mom talked about the need to be careful and alert to any unwanted behavior. They agreed that Joe would not spend time at this man's house unless his wife was also at home. The unfortunate consequence of this talk was that Joe pretty much cut off his contact with Jerry.

These are hard issues. Parents don't want to be putting fear into the minds of their children. On the other hand, young people need to recognize the potential dangers of inappropriate relationships and be encouraged to both be on their guard and talk to their parents about anything that makes them feel uncomfortable.

For discussions such as the one above, time and place are quite important. You want to be sure to have enough time to present the issue, allow time for silence and thought on the part of your child, and then time to talk. You don't want to drop an issue on them and walk away. You need to be patient with the process and willing to withstand a period of silence, even hostile silence. If they don't open up to talk about the issue, then bring it up again and keep bringing it up until they do talk. Break down the issue into smaller parts, if necessary. Or it may be necessary to frankly ask, "Has anything happened? You seem angry about this. I know it's hard to talk about but I do want to help you with it."

If they don't want to talk, ask if they would be willing to write about their feelings.

Not only time but place should be considered. The best place for such talks is in the car or while taking a walk. This way you are not face to face. It is easier to talk about difficult things when not looking at each other.

Sexually Transmitted Diseases

Sexually transmitted diseases (STD's) or infections are prevalent among those who are sexually active. (For more details, see Un-Talked-to Children Act Out Their Curiosity: STD's.) The most vulnerable are young women, who are biologically more susceptible than older women to sexually transmitted diseases or infections.[54] But teens tend to have an "It won't happen to me!" attitude. Looking back to the 1960s and the advent of the birth control pill, this youthful misconception mentally eliminated any risk of disease or pregnancy with sex outside of marriage. The burgeoning of sexually transmitted diseases was one unfortunate result.

Now, a similar attitude can be detected in the campaign to inoculate teens against Human papillomavirus (HPV). It was reported in January 2012 that nearly one in four teenage girls thought that once they had the vaccine they were protected from *all* sexually transmitted infections (STI's).[55] Further illustrating this attitude is a report from the Institute of Youth Development stating that almost half of sexually active teens think their risk of getting AIDS is zero.[56]

A lot of youthful thinking is wishful thinking. And given the fact that these diseases are often STI's (Sexually Transmitted Infections) involving people who are infected but show no manifestation of illness, youthful reasoning remains "So how could I be at risk for catching a disease? I'm not sleeping with anyone who is sick."

Cause and Effect

We learn, sometimes painfully, about the many physical laws. For example: "Don't touch the hot stove." Sometimes, in their curiosity, children *will* touch a hot stove, testing what their parents have told them. They wonder: "Is it really hot? Will it hurt me?" When they do touch the stove, they find out it hurts and won't repeat the action. Cause (touching the hot stove): effect (searing pain). To avoid pain, they quickly learn what *not* to do.

In the same way, moral laws, if ignored, cause us a great deal of pain. The difference between breaking physical laws and ignoring moral laws is that the effect or consequence of ignoring a moral law is usually greatly delayed. By the time we are hurting and in pain, we have often forgotten what act caused our pain. For example, women don't begin to confront their post-abortion feelings for an average of five years.[57] By that time, the cause of the pain is hard to remember or identify.

> *Breaking either the physical or moral laws has consequences; the only difference is the time delay after breaking moral laws.*

Ask your youth this question: "In what situation can two people have sexual contact as often as they want and never have to worry about contracting a sexually transmitted disease?"

The only one-hundred-percent way to avoid STD's is for both husband and wife to save sex until marriage and then only have sex with each other throughout their lives. God created us as a closed system. These diseases are sexually transmitted (cannot be acquired except through sexual contact); so, if you have never been exposed, you can't transmit something you don't have.

Visits to the Doctor

Because of the prevalence of sexually transmitted diseases, when your child is scheduled for a physical around age 12 to 13 some doctors may request that the accompanying parent leave the room for awhile so the medical provider can have time alone with your child. During this time, your child may be asked if he/she is sexually active, what his/her sexual preference is, and other questions about their social and home interactions. If they say that they are sexually active, birth control prescriptions and vaccines may be offered without parental consent, permission or knowledge.

Parents need to know that they do not need to leave the exam room when invited to do so. This is something that is best discussed with your child as he/she approaches age 12 to 13. It would be best if your son/daughter makes the decision as to whether or not he wants his parent to stay in the room, and even better if he/she can express his/her desire. However, if your child wants you to remain in the room but feels shy about stating their preference, you can express it for them. This is also true if your child has to go to the emergency room. You, as a parent, do not need to be out of the room during any part of their visit (except maybe for x-rays).

Social Media

Once your child involves him/herself with the various social media, they may be exposed to cyber bullying, bullying directed toward them or people they know. It's not that kids have suddenly started to be mean; no, there have always been the "playground bullies" and kids that try to gang up against an unpopular person. But once this kind of unkind behavior has gone behind the keyboard, versus face to face, it takes on a new malignancy. Gossip, unkind comments, judgments written through social media can spread rapidly and widely in cyberspace, often available for anyone to view. In general, it is a whole lot easier to make unkind remarks digitally than it is to make them face to face.

Ask yourself and your children these questions:

The 'legal age' for signing up for a Facebook account is 13. Is your 13-year-old able to make mature judgments about what to share with others and who to share it with?

Is your 13-year-old able to limit his/her time on these activities, or is it likely to take over their lives? Teenage brain research suggests that teens are still being driven by their emotions, particularly fear, rage and impulse. They are usually not capable of higher order brain functions such as reasoning, planning and judgment until their late teens or even into their 20's. Is it wise to allow full and independent access to a powerful social media which could have major consequences on their lives (to say nothing about the time they may invest to the detriment of exercise and face-to-face interaction)?

What kind of rules will there be in your family for using electronic devices? For how many hours a day/week? Any time, any place? Will you allow your children or yourselves to be texting, for example, during meals, while in a restaurant, when you have guests visiting? You may want to visit www.cpyu.org. Under "search" put in Family Digital Covenant of Conduct. Going through a contract such as this opens up meaningful communication and minimizes ongoing conflict.

How many "friends" can one handle? Friendships would better be measured in terms of quality rather than quantity.

What is a friend? How does your teen define a friend? If we are called to "rejoice with those who rejoice, [and] weep with those who weep" (Romans 12:15), what does that look like—a message on our friend's wall? When a friend is hurting, how are they most comforted: with a cyber message or a person in the flesh? Steve Marche, writing for *The Atlantic*, states: "for all this connectivity, new research suggests that we have never been lonelier (or more narcissistic)—and that this loneliness is making us mentally and physically ill."[58]

Some Thoughts

Encourage your children to interact with their friends face to face.

Encourage your children to bring their friends home. In one of the classes I taught, one person told of a wise mother who hosted a monthly tea party for her daughter and all her friends, providing a time for them to be together and chat face to face.

Use electronic communication for scheduling time and place or homework questions. Talk, communicate, interact face to face and save the electronic social media until they are older.

Chapter 7

PORNOGRAPHY

Pornography is a devastating problem exacerbated in recent years by the advent of the Internet, which allows unlimited access from millions of homes. Pornography, its prevalence, and its harm need to be an open subject from preadolescence throughout the rest of your teen's years at home. The fruit of having nurtured a close, caring, loving and trusting relationship between you and your children during their early years pays dividends now. Children/youth should now understand that the boundaries parents encourage are given for their protection. And, of course, the boundaries given need to be practiced by parents as well as their children. It's not just what you say, it is very much what you do: children/youth watch their parents to see if they practice what they preach. Parents need to model healthy Internet behavior. It would be helpful if we asked ourselves: "Would I be comfortable if everything I view or listen to were public knowledge? Are there things I want to keep private and secret?"

Prevalence of Pornography

➢ In September of 2003, 32 million different individuals visited pornographic websites during that month.[59]

- Also in 2003, 2.5 billion pornographic emails were being sent daily.[60]

- By 2010 there were 68 million requests daily for pornographic sites.[61]

- Eighty percent of kids who use the Internet receive pornographic spam daily.[62]

- *Every second*, 372 Internet users are typing adult search items.[63]

- Eighty-nine percent of pornographic web pages are produced in the United States.[64]

- Forty-seven percent of Christian families said pornography is a problem in their home.[65]

- Ninety-four percent of Americans believe a ban on Internet pornography should be legal,[66] and yet thirty-four percent of adults in the United States feel there is nothing wrong with the use of pornography.[67]

- *In 2006 it was reported that twenty percent of Christian women were addicted to pornography.*[68]

Youth and Pornography

Ninety-one percent of the first exposure by teens to pornography was during benign activities such as research for school projects or surfing the Web for other information.[69]

The majority of teenagers' online use occurs at home, right after school, when working parents are absent.[70] And because they are absent, sixty-two percent of teenagers' parents are unaware that their children have accessed objectionable websites.[71]

> The average age of first Internet exposure to pornography is nine years old.[72]

> The average age of seeking help is 30-35.[73] (That's twenty-one to twenty-six years of building an addiction!)

> Ninety percent of 8- to16-year-olds have viewed pornography.[74]

> Eighty percent of 15- to 17-year-olds have had multiple exposures to hard-core pornography.[75]

The Department of Justice warns that "never before, in the history of telecommunications media in the United States, has so much indecent (and obscene) material been so easily accessible by so many minors in so many homes with so few restrictions."[76]

Twenty percent of teens, overall, have sent or posted nude or seminude pictures or videos of themselves.[77]

Effects On Children and Adolescents

A study of youth between the ages of 10 and 17 noted a significant relationship between frequent pornography use and feelings of loneliness and major depression.[78]

> Frequent use of pornography spurs earlier onset of first sexual intercourse.[79]

> Use of pornography leads to the belief that sexual satisfaction is attainable without a committed relationship.[80]

> Pornography usage leads to the belief that being married or having a family are unattractive prospects.[81]

> ➤ Those who frequently view pornography overestimate the prevalence of less common practices like group sex, bestiality, or sadomasochistic activity.[82]

Effect on Marriage

Pornography on the Internet was cited as a significant reason for *2 out of 3 divorces.*[83] Nine to ten years ago, pornography had almost no effect on divorces.[84]

Pornography increases the risk of marital infidelity by more than 300%.[85]

Be aware of magazines and other literature which might be lying around your homes. Think of adolescents, particularly sons, who may struggle intensely with images of scantily-clothed women in magazines of any kind. It doesn't have to be *Playboy* to cause a young person to stumble.

Twelve-year-old Peter admitted to a problem with pornography and asked his parents to please not display the travel magazines in the living room. His parents were surprised and asked what problem he had with them. He opened up the magazine and showed them several images which were tempting to him. He added that his parents' help in this battle was essential to him. They immediately removed all such images from display around the house.

It is easy to lose sight of that which might be tempting to others. We need to pay careful attention to what comes into our homes and ask ourselves: "Do I really need to have this material in the house?" Also, stay in close touch with your teenagers concerning the areas in which they struggle.

Being grown up means being willing to be "my brother's keeper" (Genesis 4:9b). One of our jobs as parents is to be gatekeepers during our children's growing up years, shielding them, as much as possible, from the temptations that are flagrant in our culture.

Some Guiding Principles

It is impossible for parents to keep children away from all tempting images—they are just too prevalent. But working together, parents can guide their children and keep nudging them toward the right path.

As soon as your children can access the Internet on their own (by early in adolescence), talk to them about pornography: what it is, how prevalent it is, and how damaging it can be. Encourage them to come to you if they find themselves struggling with pornography of any kind. Let them know that if they find themselves attracted to it, the sooner they get help the better. As already noted, the average age of first exposure to pornography is *nine years old*. The average age of dealing with it is 35-36 years of age.[86] Ingrained habits (fostered over many years) are harder to break than a recently-acquired one.

Create an atmosphere that allows for confession. An atmosphere of condemnation and judgment does not lend itself to confession. If parents are open about their own failings, children will be more apt to confess their struggles.

Don't over-react. Be sad, but not mad. If your teens admit to a problem with pornography, they are dealing with a very powerful pull and they need a lot of loving, patient, consistent, long-term help.

If they admit to being troubled by pornography, a good first question to ask is, "How can I best help you with this?" They may be able to tell you what kind of boundaries they need. Keep close to them on this, checking in often with the question, "How are you doing with your struggle against pornography?"

Ask them to think about who's behind the pictures, moving them from their fantasy conjured up by pornographic images to the reality of the one who is pictured. "Who is that person, really? What is their life like? How do these graphic, degrading pictures affect their life? What if that was your sister/friend/cousin?"

Think about Psalm 139:13-14: God made our bodies. He made them truly beautiful to reflect Him and His love for us. How do pornographic images fit into "fearfully and wonderfully made" (Psalm 139:14)?

Help your kids to understand that pornography can affect brain chemistry and wear away at how the brain is designed to respond to sex, chemically diluting the future joy and pleasure that sex can have when used as God designed it.

Ask what triggers they can identify: images or places that start their mind down the pornographic road. Work together to eliminate these triggers.

In his struggle with pornography, one adolescent stated that just walking by a store like Victoria's Secret started the images rolling. He learned to walk by the store looking the other way or avoid passing by the store, when possible. Another young man, for a time, found it too tempting to check out of a grocery store—too many tabloids with suggestive pictures. He asked his friends, or parents, to get what he needed.

Encourage hobbies, sports, reading of great literature, listening to good music, or other interests. Limit alone time and fill up idle time! What devices in your home access the Internet? Carefully consider where they are located and when and where they can be used.

Internet Safety

For younger children, some form of "Internet Nanny" might be helpful. These products allow Internet filtering, parental monitors, and maps as to what sites have been accessed. At least one parent needs to be computer-savvy. If not, educate yourself.

Talk about appropriate sites. Permanently block all incoming spam that even hints at pornography. Keep computers and all Internet devices as family tools in common areas. Know what your kids are doing on the Internet. Know their Internet friends. Know their passwords. Set reasonable guidelines and monitor these to be certain they are followed.

Phones and Other Internet Devices

If they have a phone, does it have to have all the bells and whistles? If you are going to give your adolescent a phone, consider a basic model that only makes and receives calls. Also, be prepared to monitor the use of any other devices which your adolescents have which can access the Web.

Home Alone

In early adolescence Jacob was shown a *Playboy* centerfold at the home of a friend. That was all it took to initiate a battle. For a time he fought this battle in secret; but all too frequently, when he was home alone, he'd give in to the temptation of the Internet or the television.

His parents noticed a deterioration in his behavior. He was spending more and more time alone in his room. He'd come home from school, slam the door to his bedroom, and wouldn't talk. His parents knew something was wrong and began to look for an opportunity to discuss his behavior.

One day, Jacob's mom needed to run an errand in a town about 45 minutes away and asked if Jacob wanted to ride along. Usually the answer was no. (He didn't like running errands.) But this day he said yes.

They began driving and talking. The talk soon turned to pornography and how bad it was. In the midst of the conversation Jacob exploded with a vehement amount of righteous judgment: "I can't believe what's available on the Internet!"

His mom was silent for a bit, then quietly asked, "Do you have a problem with this?"

Jacob immediately broke down and started to sob. He admitted to a problem which had been getting worse for the past several months. He told his mom that it was the TV and the Internet that were his stumbling blocks. Jacob and his mom prayed, asking for forgiveness, for help to truly repent of this obsession, and for wisdom to know how best to turn away from this addiction.

His mom asked if she could share their conversation with Jacob's dad. Jacob agreed, and the three of them worked together. When asked what help he needed, Jacob said that he needed to have the computer password changed so he couldn't log on. He also asked for a lock to be put on the television to prevent his watching when home alone. Soon, he said that not only did he need to be logged onto the Web by one of his parents, but he also needed one of his parents to be near while he was accessing the Internet.

His parents stayed aware of the problem, kept checking in with him, and helped by monitoring and holding him accountable through the rest of middle school and high school. When Jacob got to college, he cultivated some close male friends, all of whom agreed to hold each other accountable. By college, his internal controls had been firmly established.

Are your children going to be home alone? Discuss boundaries— possibly an Internet lock or a password change as well as an agreement about Internet usage. For example, the Internet is only to be used when a parent is home to monitor. Don't underestimate the pull of this temptation. If your children are home alone, no matter how trustworthy they seem, they need to have blocks and boundaries in place for their safety.

In his early high school years, Jim was shown some pornographic pictures by a friend. That began the struggle for him. He did not confess this right away, but came to his mother several times in great distress, complaining about the nasty pop-ups on his computer. Finally, he confessed the problem, and he and his mom have begun to battle this together with a combination of internal and external monitoring. They realize that it will be a long battle, but they are prepared to stay the course.

Involvement with pornography is not cured overnight. Many say it is a lifetime struggle. Encourage as much accountability as possible: peers, parents, other adults. Keep loving, keep praying, keep asking, keep talking.

The goal of parental monitoring is to move children from external monitoring (imposed mechanically or by others) to internal monitoring.

External monitoring can be relaxed as they are able to set their own boundaries and act on their internal restraints. It is a cooperative effort. If they are not working with you and you try to exclusively monitor externally, they will find ways around the restraints. For example, every Internet blocking mechanism or program has ways in which such blocks can be overridden. If teens don't want to change, they will only pay lip service to what you say. Keep praying and keep persistent in your love of them.

The middle school years herald many changes: physical, emotional, intellectual and spiritual. These years are often a challenge. These are also the years when peers become very important, so get to know your children's friends. Keep close with your middle school children and nurture their trust. Be real with them, enjoy them, have fun with them, and stay connected.

Chapter 8

TEENS

Teens may look grown up on the outside but their brains are still developing, so they're still in need of regular guidance.

For some, the teenage years storm in. Your child turns from a sweet, cooperative, happy, compliant child to a monster: totally unpredictable, questioning everything, raging one moment and gentle and happy the next. One moment they act like the happy-go-lucky children they have always been, the next they are out of control. They may look all grown up, but that's just from the outside.

It used to be thought that once our children were inhabiting an adult body, they were adults. It also used to be felt that the brain was pretty much formed by age three. We, as parents, were told "let them make their own decisions; get out of their lives, they've grown up."

Since the release of new teenage brain research in 1997, we now know that, although grown up on the outside, inside teens often react as if they were still children. The research shows that the teenage brain is only about 80 percent developed in many adolescents. At the beginning of puberty, it's as if a whole bunch of grey matter is deposited in the brain. It is the task of adolescence to get that grey matter connected to the higher brain or the prefrontal cortex, a task which definitely can be assisted by parents. This last section of the brain to develop is the prefrontal cortex, home of three major functions of adult processing: reasoning, planning and judgment. That process of connectedness, or brain development, may not happen for some until the mid- to late twenties.[87]

The teenager is all too often responding to the amygdale—home of the primal feelings of fear, rage and impulse. Think about this when evaluating their behavior. Barbara Cooke, in her work on the teenage brain, gives the following description of some teenagers:

> Parents watch their teens whiz through life manipulated by the wild whims of the amygdale, home to the primal feelings such as fear, rage and impulse. And to complicate things even more, the amygdale gangs up with all kinds of hormones, and pumps them through puberty-ravaged bodies, making them moody, unpredictable, and seemingly irrational.[88]

Consider the following examples of behaviors demonstrating a lack of "upper brain" reasoning that made the news: "Two teen girls were struck by a car after they dozed off while sunbathing on a rural road in Pennsylvania." The girls were 13.[89] "Car Surfing: A Deadly Trend." (Car surfing is riding on the top of a moving vehicle: starting out lying down, then trying to stand up, all while the car continues to move.) The article describes this and other risky activities like "'ghost riding' with no one behind the wheel and 'skitching'—riding a skateboard pulled by a moving vehicle."[90]

So what's a parent to do? It has been suggested by Barbara Cooke that parents need to be the DPC for their adolescents: the Designated Prefrontal Cortex. "Dispense common sense, guidance, and advice. In other words, don't just walk away from your teen and think that he or she is ready to make all the decisions without your input."[91] Stay with them. They want you around even though they will not tell you that; instead, they will often tell you just the opposite: "I don't need your help. I can do it on my own. Get out of my life!" Don't believe them!

David Urion, an associate professor of neurology, adds: "[Wise parents] offer practical strategies for making in-the-moment decisions, rather than merely lecturing teens about the behaviors themselves."[92]

Empathize with them. Let them know that you understand how hard it is to behave in a way that is different from much of their peer group. But help them to think through the consequences of acting in irresponsible ways (drinking, sex, fast driving, skipping homework, or chronic sleep deprivation).

Help them get organized. Think of ways that will work for them to remember what needs to be done. Help them to think through when and how other activities impact those things that have to happen: school assignments, commitments, and sleep needs.

Be there for them—don't just assume that, since they tend to spend little time face-to-face with you, they don't need you to be around. Just your presence near them is helpful and encouraging to them. As has been said before, they won't tell you this until much later in their lives; but then, they are apt to thank you for being available to them through those stormy adolescent years.

Have a sense of humor. This is an important aspect of our relations with each other. Don't take yourself too seriously. Life incorporates much hilarity, so bring it out, major in it. All of this helps connect the grey matter to the higher brain or prefrontal cortex.

Additional Developmental Stage—Really?

At a 2010 youth symposium held at Gordon College in Wenham, Massachusetts, Dr. Cheryl Crawford, Assistant Professor of Youth Ministry at Azusa Pacific University, sited the work of J.J. Arnett who adds a new stage to human development called "emerging adulthood." He has written much about what seems to be a trend toward prolonged adolescence. The stages of human development, according to Arnett, are: infant, child, adolescent, emerging adult, adult. Adolescence begins at puberty (age 11 or 12) and lasts until around 18. He labels from 18 to 25 as emerging adulthood. Finally, after age 25, he believes one moves toward adulthood. This prolonged adolescence seems to be a phenomenon only seen in industrialized countries, places where young people are encouraged to explore possibilities without taking on the corresponding responsibilities.[93]

The job of the adolescent, according to Dr. Crawford, should be processing the question, "Who am I?" Arnett breaks this process of identity exploration into three areas: love, work and worldview. This processing work used to be done in the high school years, with the young person going to college having a pretty good idea of their own identity. More and more, this kind of processing is being put off into the college years or even beyond. When students arrive at college without the identity piece in place, they face tremendous loneliness. They no longer have the support of parents, the church and other adult mentors. Since their identity formation was not completed in high school, the continuing process now lacks the wisdom, leading, counsel and modeling of invested adults. Rather, the work of identity formation easily gets clothed in what is popular—peers become the models for each other and what is popular and "in" is what they identify with.[94]

A historic perspective tells us that, throughout a good portion of human history, only two stages of human development were identified: child and adult. One was considered an adult when one went through puberty. Most people, by the age of 14 or 15, were working or had a good deal of responsibility within their families. Sometimes they were married and soon to be parents.

The concept of a teenager is only about 70 years old, first used somewhere between 1938 and 1941. Modern youth have many of the desires and abilities of an adult without the responsibilities and expectations. They have money to spend, freedom from chores and responsibilities, and a means of transportation. A car and license, in particular, give a sense of freedom unencumbered by oversight or guidance from parents who no longer know where their children are, who they are with, or even when to expect them back.

Responsibility plays an important part in a young person's moving into adulthood. According to Arnett's research, young people feel they are adults when they accept responsibility for themselves, start making independent decisions, and become financially independent. Those who had a child, on the other hand, felt that parenthood was the marker of having entered adulthood.[95] Too often the modern concept of adolescence "allows, encourages, and even trains young people to remain childish for much longer than necessary."[96]

Is the research accurate that shows the connections to the frontal lobe not being completed until the mid- to late twenties? Do we really need to add a new stage to human development? Or, is this research simply descriptive of where we are today: a culture that demands little of adolescents, gives them what they think they want, and requires no accountability?

Adolescents who are encouraged and expected to exercise and practice the frontal lobe activities of reasoning, planning and judgment *do* move forward in these tasks, making connections to the higher brain and stimulating neural pathways to the prefrontal cortex. This work helps the young person toward the completion of the adult brain connections at ages similar to what has been observed in the past.[97]

Decision Making

Thoughtful decision making exercises the frontal lobe, so encourage your young person to be intentional about their choices. It may be helpful to pull apart the decision-making process using the following eight steps:

1. Define the decision.
2. Identify goals.
3. Consider alternative courses of action (all the different decisions you could make).
4. Consider the consequences of each alternative.
5. Ask advice. Get input from those you trust: peers, parents and other adults.

6. Choose one of the alternatives.

7. Try out this course of action.

8. Rethink your choice, if necessary.

Chapter 9

HIGH SCHOOL

"In my day, 'STD' stood for 'Stay Together Dang it' "

The Proper Place for Sex

By the time teens are in high school, renew discussions about the purpose of sex, dealing with sexual feelings, and dating. Sex is a wonderfully fun, joy-filled, good gift of God when used as it was designed. But we experience strong (at times extremely strong) sexual urges before and outside of marriage. How can we prepare our kids to deal with those?

Careful thought needs to go into how to frame conversations and discussions about sex that will guide teens toward an elevated view of their sexuality. You've talked about the pitfalls of early sex, STD's, and pornography, all of which are the negatives of sex; now it's time to talk about the positives and the great advantages of saving sex until marriage. Find out from your teen what they want sex to mean in their lives. Ask them, "What have you heard us say about sex?" Use open-ended questions; don't get uncomfortable with silence; wait for them to respond. You can refine your questions depending on how they answer.

Ask them what's wrong with this logic: "Don't have sex until you're married; but if you do, be sure to use protection." Encourage their answer, then emphasize that sex is about more than safety, more than 'being ready,' more than my pleasure/satisfaction. Sex is about a lifelong relationship: faithfulness, fidelity, knowing, commitment, and loyalty.

Have your teen articulate the reasons why God gave such a wonderful gift but then said to use it only in marriage. If they can't give the reasons, go back and review these with them and, together, develop a plan of action to help maintain their purity. (See Chapter 13 for discussion of the reasons why God gave sex to be used only in marriage.)

Remind them that sex cannot be separated from relationship. If it is, it falls far short of the possible pleasure and joy. Remind them that marriage is not for everyone; maybe they will remain single and never marry. Assure them that singleness is OK with you. You will be talking with them about dating and the proper place for sex, but that doesn't mean that your ultimate hope for them is that they marry. Hopefully, you are demonstrating to them that your ultimate expectation for them is that they will lead fulfilled, God-honoring lives no matter where that takes them. Sex is not a given of life. All too often it is assumed that sex is "necessary to be truly, fully alive."[98] It isn't. Jesus abstained all of His life and He was certainly fully alive. Hear the Apostle Paul: "I wish that all were as I myself am. But each has his own gift from God, one of one kind and one of another. To the unmarried and the widows I say that it is good for them to remain single as I am" (1 Corinthians 7:7-8).

Age of Single Dating/% Sexually Involved[99]

Age of Single Dating	% having sex before HS Graduation
12 Years Old	91%
13 Years Old	56%
14 Years Old	53%
15 Years Old	40%
16 Years Old	20%

Give the subject of dating a good deal of thought before your teens ask about it. You and your spouse decide: Will you allow your teens to date? How do you and they define dating? How will you and your teens decide what age dating will be allowed? Will it be a chronological age or will you (parents) need to see some demonstration of maturity on the part of your adolescent before dating is allowed? What does maturity look like? Should women initiate a date or just men? If you think that men should be the initiators, how does a woman show she's interested? If dating will be allowed, are there alternatives to single dating?

Single dating assumes that the couple spends a good deal of time alone, focused on each other. The earlier single dating starts, the greater the temptation to move forward on the physical continuum. Although it is wise to discourage early single dating, it is also wise not to discourage and deny a relationship between two who are young but attracted to each other. Think about inviting the girl/boyfriend into your home. Include them in your family activities and, at times, include the family of the girl/boyfriend too.

Going Steady

Pairing off seems to be a serial sort of thing. They date, get to know one another, and grow close to each other until some problem develops or the romance starts to fade, at which point they break up and look for a new dating relationship. In his book *I Kissed Dating Good-bye*, Josh Harris suggests that the way we date prepares us more for divorce than marriage.[100] Can our young people spend more time in groups and reject the mentality of pairing off?

The Dating Pyramid

This pyramid represents a broad foundation upon which to base a marriage.

Marry

Become Engaged

Select a few with whom to go steady

Select a few friends to date

Friendships with lots of people

Groups Rather than Single Dates

Being together in a group has some distinct advantages. Groups could include youth group, well-supervised parties, time with family members, or other gatherings (again, well-supervised when young teens are involved). Let's say that Sue is interested in John. In a group she gets to observe him interacting with a lot of others. In a group he is not necessarily on his best behavior, but is more apt to be himself. He is not likely to be polished, the way he might be on an exclusive date. In groups, Sue can see how John treats others, how he reacts in different situations: Is he focused on himself or others? Does he have a sense of humor or does he take himself too seriously? On an exclusive date, John is apt to control situations to show himself at his best. And, of course, all of the above is true if it were John who was interested in Sue.

A young couple, out of college, went on a skiing date with a group. Later, on the way back to the ski club cabin, the guy said: "Let's not go back for a bit so we don't have to help with dinner." That told her a lot about this young man's character and focus. She did not date him again.

On another ski retreat, two young people were on a chair lift near the top when they noticed some children who had gotten stuck in some deep snow. The guy suggested they go and see if they could help. This told the young woman a good deal about this young man's character. She did date him again.

Bringing Friends Home

Encourage your teens to bring friends home (when you are present, of course). Our guard is down on home turf, so for a teen to have a girl/boyfriend at their home without parents present is an unwise choice: no supervision, no accountability, yet in comfortable, familiar surroundings.

Mary got a phone call from her high school son, Terry, asking with some exasperation:

"Are you finally home?"

"Yes," replied Mary. "What's up?"

Terry explained that he and Christine had been driving around for the last hour trying to find a well-supervised place just to spend time together. Both his parents and hers were not home and, being a holiday, the libraries were closed.

Mary encouraged them to come on home. It pleased Mary to get this phone call from Terry because it reinforced his responsibility and maturity in her mind: he knew that it was not wise for he and Christine to spend time alone together and he certainly knew not to go to either home unless a parent was present.

Try to make your home attractive to your kids' friends. Encourage games, watching movies together as a family with friends, singing together, eating together, and just living life at your home with their friends.

Suggesting this to your teen may initially be met with resistance. However, they may well bring it up again, this time as their idea.

This happened in our home when I suggested to our son that he organize a game of Capture the Flag. At first he shot the idea down, but later asked if he could do just that. He is a terrific organizer and soon had a monthly or bi-monthly game going after dark on our property. This had a life of its own and, before he graduated from high school, we had over 100 kids playing the game. Our son had strict rules which were carefully laid out: signing in by name with emergency phone numbers noted, no alcohol, reporting the intent to leave, and signing out. Interest spread through word of mouth, so we didn't always personally know the youth who came. One day, our son overheard the following conversation between two young men he did not know:

"Hey, you want to go to the Joneses' tonight to play Capture the Flag?"

"Yeah, I've heard they have a lot of fun. I'll bring a 6-pack."

"Oh, no you won't," replied his friend. "No booze allowed, and they check! Let's just go and have fun with the game."

Another family began encouraging an afternoon tea at their home with their daughter and several of her friends. This started when she was younger but continued for a number of years, giving friends a place to safely hang out to just talk and be girls.

Do your friends have children/teens the same age as your own? Orchestrate lots of interaction with those families both with the whole family and, at times, just with the teens. Take Sue and John again as an example. Being in each other's homes allows John to observe the interaction Sue has with her parents, and vice versa. What type of relationship do they have? It also allows parents to observe Sue and John together and interacting with the rest of the family.

Supervision

Young people seldom feel they need supervision. When I was teaching 7th grade, I gave my students some questions on supervision. They were to look at several activities and decide if an activity was appropriate or inappropriate for them as 7th graders. Then I sent the same questions home for their parents to answer. Here are two of the questions and their answers.

Go to co-ed parties without adult supervision:

    Students - 60% answered "appropriate"

    Parents - 100% answered "inappropriate"

Boy/girl home alone together without parent:

> Students - 86% answered "appropriate"
>
> Parents - 97% answered "inappropriate"

Finally, I sent both papers home, the student answers and the parent answers, and suggested parents and students talk over their differences. Try this activity yourself. Ask your teens to answer questions. You do the same, then exchange answers and talk about the differences in perspective. This could be a good time to ask what they have heard you say about sex and to articulate why God gave the gift of sex only for marriage.

Don't back off from your supervision until your teen consistently demonstrates responsible and mature behavior. Nevertheless, as long as you are living together as a family, it only makes sense that each one know the four "W's" about each other: where, what, when and with whom? "Where are you going? What are you planning? When will you be back? Who are you going with?"

Curfews

Curfews should take into account the maturity and responsibility of your teen, the obligations he/she has (homework and other engagements the next day), sleep needs, and the particular activity involved. For example, if Sue and John are going to a movie that is over at 9:30, would their desire to stay out until midnight be wise? In talking over curfews, fit them to the activities. Discourage down time—time without anything planned. Down time is best spent in a well-supervised place.

Teens do have strong sexual feelings. Many in our culture would encourage the expression and satisfaction of these sexual urges as often as and with whomever they please. However, this random and rampant expression will not lead to fulfillment. Rather, too often such encounters result in heartbreak, disease, loneliness and pain. So, how do we deal with all the sexual energy and feelings engendered during the single years?

Chapter 10

DEALING WITH SEXUAL FEELINGS

Of the ten commandments, which one do we disobey first? The tenth: "You shall not covet..."(Exodus 20:17a). Coveting is wanting something which is not yours. Coveting is done with our brains. Disobedience starts with our thoughts.

God gave us sexual appetites, but our appetites need to be controlled. We *can* control what we think about! When thoughts of an unhealthy nature enter our brains, think about what the Apostle Paul tells us: "Finally, brothers, whatever is true, whatever is honorable, whatever is just, whatever is pure, whatever is lovely, whatever is commendable, if there is any excellence, if there is anything worthy of praise, think about these things" (Philippians 4:8).

Develop a discipline of taking each of the things the Apostle Paul suggests and putting flesh on them. For example, what things have you heard today that are "true"? What is truth? What does it mean to be "honorable"? Did you see it modeled today? Think about all the lovely things you can. By the time you finish with the apostle's list you will have successfully steered your mind away from unhealthy thoughts...until the next time.

Sexual Arousal Continuum

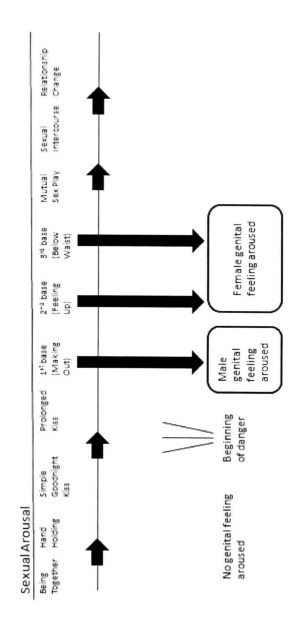

Continuum of Sexual Arousal

Young people need to understand that men and women are very different when it comes to sexual arousal. One cannot judge the potential for arousal based on one's own feelings—we are made too differently. In general, men are aroused much sooner than women, so if a woman is judging the time to disengage from physical activity based on her own feelings, she may be surprised and not understand why the man finds it extremely difficult to stop.

Women need to understand what stimulates them, and they also need to know what stimulates men. And men need to understand the same about women. (See Sexual Arousal Continuum chart on facing page.)

Male Arousal

Most men are aroused by three things. Pay attention—these are hard to remember: *what they see...what they see...and what they see!*

Understanding this, discuss with your daughters what implications this has on the clothes they wear. They probably want to dress as others do, to wear the "in" thing, the cool thing. "Am I my brother's keeper?" they may ask, denying responsibility for others' reactions. What they should ask is: "Am I willing to help my male friends/acquaintances by *not* dressing in a provocative way?" One male Christian writer put it this way: "When Christian women 'dress modestly' they show love for their male neighbors, realizing the visual temptation offered by female contours."[101] Ask your daughters to accept responsibility for the effect clothing (or lack thereof) has on men. Ask them to think through the difference between dowdy and

105

sexy. Does a middle ground exist? Ask them to differentiate between sexy and attractive.

> ### *Men are aroused by what they see,*
> ### *by what they see, and by what they see!*

Daughters do well to use their fathers or brothers as their measuring stick and should check with Dad as to the appropriateness of the way they dress. One father tells of how his daughter questions him before she leaves for school: "What do you think, Dad?" All he has to do is shake his head ("No") and she returns to her room to rectify her dress.

The goal, of course, is not to make this a daily battle but to have developed such a close and caring relationship that daughters value Dad's opinion and are willing to follow his lead. We probably all know of young women who are told, "You will *not* leave this house dressed like that!" They change, but carry the offending garment in their backpacks only to change back as soon as they get to school. "Rules without relationships lead to rebellion."[102]

Female Arousal

Women are aroused by what they hear and by relationships. Understanding this, encourage your sons to be mindful of what they say to women. How do they sign off an email or Facebook communication? Do they use the word "love"? It may seem innocent to a young man, but to a young woman it may have deeper connotations than a guy intends.

Girls have a tendency to magnify something said by a boy they like to prove that "he *really* likes me." Since, in general, women tend to interpret male behavior to fit their hopes/dreams, men need to be careful that nothing they say or do encourages a girl if they are really not interested. Just trying to be nice can add fuel to a woman's fire. Be polite and courteous, but don't respond to flirtation. And never tell a woman that you love her unless you are in a position to move the relationship forward toward marriage. Unfortunately, and rather cruelly, a man can push a woman toward sex by claiming "I love you." She thinks: He said he loves me...he must mean he plans to marry me...so it must be OK.

Here are some other 'come-on lines' used by someone who wants to further a physical relationship when the other person is reluctant:

- ➤ "You would if you really loved me."
- ➤ "Everyone does it."
- ➤ "Don't you trust me?"
- ➤ "If it feels good, do it."
- ➤ "We've come this far, so why not?"
- ➤ "Don't you think it's time?"
- ➤ "You don't think I'm good enough for you?"
- ➤ "What's a marriage certificate anyway?"
- ➤ "Can't you think for yourself?"
- ➤ "Do it for me."
- ➤ "Nobody's going to stop us."
- ➤ "You mean you haven't tried it before?"
- ➤ "What's the matter with you?"
- ➤ "I'll tell everyone that you didn't."
- ➤ "You say you don't want to, but I know what you really want."

Share these lines (or others you think of) with your teen and ask him/her to think of a gentle response to each of them, basically saying "No, I don't want to go there."

Because women are aroused by what they hear and relationship, men should be sensitive to what their female friends and acquaintances might be hearing and ask themselves the question: "Am I helping to protect my 'sister' for the man she will eventually marry?"

Women are aroused by what they hear and by relationship.

At the right side of the continuum it reads: "Relationship Change." Once sex has occurred within a relationship, the relationship does change. Dave Carder, in his book *Close Calls*, says: "The relationship stops growing once it becomes sexual, because the erotic aspect will become the primary focus of [the couple's] time together."[103] Further, in a relationship between adolescents, the couple is apt to break up after sex occurs. Sixty-one percent of teens break up within three months after initiating sex; eighty percent break up within six months. This often is a very painful consequence, especially for young women.

One might think that a kiss is well back on the physical/emotional continuum. It depends on what kind of a kiss it is. When asked the purpose of a kiss, a group of adults responded:

➢ To show affection
➢ To say 'I love you' (chaste kiss)

➤ To say 'I want you' (unchaste kiss)

➤ The first step toward sexual intercourse—if I had been asked this many years ago, I would not have thought this; now I know.

Our physical bodies, decoupled from an ethical compass, drive toward the right side of the continuum, often resulting in intended or unintended sexual involvement. Each couple, as they move forward in their relationship, needs to think about where their boundaries lie. Does it take physical expression to prove that you care for or love someone?

One couple decided to set their guardrail on the physical continuum to the left of kissing—they wanted their first kiss to be at the altar. At the end of their wedding ceremony one of their guests asked: "But how did she know that he loved her?"

Answer: "He told her."

Actions speak louder than words, we're told; but sometimes, words are safer and more appropriate.

Relationships which lead to marriage need a broad foundation: intellectual, social, emotional, spiritual and physical. It takes precious little time to develop a physical relationship. Building the broad foundation for a life together, however, entails carefully-structured activities and a lot of time.

I'm 25 years old.... When you mention the word 'virgin' in everyday conversation, more often than not, the image that pops up is a repressed super-nerd bumbling his way to decades of sexual frustration. But that's not me. My chastity is not the product of unresolved Freudian fears—it is the result of [a] conscious decision, coupled with years of hard labor.

Two years ago, I met Sonja (we plan to be married in June...). You'd think our relationship would be lacking. No sex, no love, right? In our case, however, it's had the opposite effect. We both made individual decisions to abstain. As a couple, we've had the chance to support each other in the quest to remain virgins until marriage. Instead of becoming a wall between us, this bit of team play has brought us close. We spend less time in the bedroom and more time together learning about each other, sharing hopes and dreams.... Our lack of intimacy has led to, well, more intimacy than I could have hoped for.[104]

Don't Be Alone Together

Don't be alone together, at least not until you have both clearly established your boundaries and trust each other to uphold them. Being alone together turns the focus to each other, which usually leads to more and more physical behavior. The presence of others stimulates conversation, broadens the interactions, and changes the focus.

Be Where You Should Be

This principle is illustrated in 2 Samuel 11: "In the spring of the year, the time when kings go off to battle, David sent Joab and his servants with him, and all Israel.... But David remained in Jerusalem" (2 Sam 11:1).

The text doesn't tell us why David stayed behind, but it is clear that by remaining in Jerusalem his accountability group was gone. All his friends and colleagues had gone off to war. One can speculate that David soon became bored. Had he read through all the books available, watched all the latest DVD's, gotten tired of Solitaire? In any case, we're told: "late one afternoon, when David arose from his couch and was walking on the roof of the king's house" he saw a beautiful woman (2 Sam 11:2). Never mind that she was the wife of a good friend. He saw her, he called for her, and he had sex with her.

Had David been where he should have been this never would have happened. If he had been doing what kings did in the spring, he would have been with his friend, not with his friend's wife.

Be Aware of Expectations

If a woman agrees to go out to dinner with a man, she is in no way obligated to go home with him just because he may have bought her an expensive dinner. The reverse is also true. Warn your teens that they only agree to what they agree to. They do not need to concern themselves with hidden expectations and they have no obligation or need to fulfill someone else's agenda.

This is a good verse to keep in mind: "Do not be conformed to this world, but be transformed by the renewal of your mind, that by testing you may discern what is the will of God, what is good and acceptable and perfect" (Romans 12:2).

The expectations that kids need to be aware of are the expectations of their parents and those of their Lord, not someone that wants something from them. Encourage your kids to hold fast to what they commit to and feel obligated to nothing more.

Be Prepared to Flee

If your teen finds him/herself close to a compromising situation, they need to get away. *Always assure your children that, no matter where they are or what time it is, if they need rescue, you'll come.*

Joseph in Potiphar's house is a really good example of knowing when to flee.

> Now Joseph was handsome in form and appearance. And after a time his master's wife cast her eyes on Joseph and said, 'Lie with me!' But he refused… And as she spoke to Joseph day after day, he would not listen to her, to lie beside her or to be with her. But one day, when he went into the house to do his work and none of the men of the house was there in the house, she caught him by his garment, saying, 'Lie with me.' But he left his garment in her hand and fled and got out of the house. (Genesis 39:6b-12)

Notice that Joseph would not listen to her, lie beside her, or even "be with her." He tried everything to shake her interest in him. He was honest with her, he was honest with himself, but finally it became clear that nothing was left except to flee the situation. How easy it would have been for Joseph to have rationalized an affair with this powerful woman. Had he agreed to sleep with her, he probably could have talked her into seeing that he got a big boost into a political career. After all, his early dreams indicated that he was to become a somebody with lots of authority. How easy for him to think this must be the way God intended for him to go. Instead, he says:

"How then can I do this great wickedness and sin against God?" Joseph refused to rationalize his position, and so he fled.

It is important to realize that doing the right thing does not always bring a happy ending. Sometimes the results, at least immediately, can be painful. Joseph was accused by Potiphar's wife of attempted rape and was promptly sent to prison where he remained for several years. In that culture it would not have been unreasonable to expect a death sentence with the accusation. Potiphar was merciful (or he knew better than to trust the account of his wife).

Bottom line: there are times when the only thing to do is to flee.

Accountability

Accountability is key for anyone trying to live an ethical and upright life. Choosing to be accountable reminds us we're sinful human beings but also offers the support of others who share the same struggles. There are many tools available today to help with accountability and some of them are surprisingly concrete.

One might think about a questionnaire, a contract, a ring or a cross. The purpose for all of these is to remind teens of their commitment to sexual purity. It may be helpful to ask your teen(s) to answer written questions as they think through their thoughts and feelings about dating. Together, you and your teen may decide to use a dating contract. Following is an example of a high school student and her boyfriend who decided to use this method of accountability.

I met my future husband when I was fifteen years old, a freshman in high school. Although I wasn't allowed to officially date until I was sixteen, we decided to draw up a contract outlining our physical standards. We chose a few Scripture verses that we wanted to strive to live toward and had our parents and mentors sign the contract. We are very thankful that we drew up that contract for a couple of reasons. It allowed us the opportunity to communicate clearly about our standards. And we had the opportunity to show our parents that we were serious about honoring one another. However, the contract was not a magic ticket to easy purity! If anything, we realized how many gray areas there are in a physical relationship, and how important it is to have both individuals' hearts aligned with the Lord.

We allowed this contract to influence and guide us throughout our dating years.

A promise ring, a cross, or some other tangible piece of jewelry is another possibility. These are available in most Christian book stores or online. If this is something you choose to do, make a big deal of the presentation: maybe take your teen out for a really special (adult) dinner. Consider writing them a letter including things about your joy when they were first born, your dreams for their future, your encouragement for them to remain sexually abstinent until marriage, and your promise to walk with them throughout their single years.

Jerry asked for a cross. He picked it out and his parents gave it to him after a time of prayer and talking about the seriousness of his commitment. He wore it next to his skin and knew that if he ever decided to violate his promise, the cross would be the last item to be removed and a potent reminder of what he was about to do. He wore it faithfully until his wedding day.

Accountability helps to lessen the potential dangers of rationalization. Our minds can lead us into all kinds of things that are not healthy or good, and yet we convince ourselves that nothing is wrong with what we're thinking. When we keep to ourselves and ask counsel of no one, we are very vulnerable to the deception of our own rationalization. We need to seek God's wisdom in our thinking and measure our thoughts according to His Word. And we need to be sharing our thinking with good friends and/or parents face-to-face. Often, just by sharing aloud with another, we hear our rationalization and self-correct.

Mary had been happily married for several years when she was sent by her church to a seminar in a distant city. She flew to the seminar with a woman friend but the return trip was with a man from the congregation also sent to the seminar. While waiting at the airport the few hours until their plane left, Mary and Mike began to share their life stories. Mike had some sad issues in his life and, as he shared his story, Mary responded with great empathy. They suddenly found themselves drawn together emotionally. (Note: The tracks of compassion can all too easily cross with the tracks of intimacy; without extreme care this could lead to illicit relationships.)

Mary and Mike began to think about each other and made efforts to be together whenever possible. This was usually at (good) church activities; none-the-less it was clear that something (not good) was going on in their heads. Mary kept these thoughts and feeling to herself until one day, talking to a close girlfriend, they got on the subject of extra-marital male/female relationships. Mary told her girlfriend about her feelings for Mike but attempted to rationalize them, to sanitize her feelings and make them seem OK. Finally, she heard herself, stopped rationalizing, and came clean with her friend. She confessed to emotional adultery, both to the Lord and (harder still) to her husband. It turned out that, though she thought she had kept her feelings private, her husband had been aware of the attraction. This had hurt him, but after she confessed, he quickly forgave her. Talking aloud about the situation removed the allure of its secrecy; confessing it allowed for resolution and restored relationship.

In trying to determine what the Lord's will is, we can think of a three-legged stool. One leg is our study of *Scripture*, God's Word which tells us His will. The second leg is *prayer*, as we earnestly come before the Lord asking for guidance and confessing our sins. The third leg is *accountability* with at least one other who really cares for us (children/teens with their parents or same-sex friends). This was certainly helpful to Jacob and his issue with pornography. (See Home Alone in Chapter 7.)

Accountability may come from unexpected sources so encourage your children to nurture close and caring face-to-face (not just digital) friendships. These should be friends with whom they can be open and who understand their convictions, even though they may not share them.

Janet shared about her 15-year-old daughter, Tara, who had strong Christian convictions and planned to save sex until marriage. Tara was very open about all of her beliefs. One day a few of her friends were talking with her and one of them said: "Tara, we really respect your commitment to remain a virgin 'till you marry. We just want you to know, if you ever get tempted to move away from that standard, please call on us. We don't agree with what you believe, but we want to help you hold to your convictions." Later, one of those friends asked to go to youth group with her.

To illustrate the power of accountability (or lack thereof), consider this story told by Ravi Zacharias in his book *Deliver Us From Evil*:

A young couple had been married some years ago. They represented every ideal worth emulating. They embodied excellence to the youth of the church. Both were preparing to practice medicine and were on sizable merit scholarships. As the pastor left the church after their wedding he rehearsed in his mind the grand occasion it had been; in all his years of ministry he had not seen a more radiant couple. He thrilled at the prospect of all that lay ahead of them.

But then, like a shattered dream, only a few months into the marriage came a dreadful awakening. In the predawn hours of a wintry night the pastor's telephone rang, and a distraught voice begged him to come. The caller, the young man of such promise, kept stuttering the words, "I think I've killed her! I think I've killed her!" The minister hastily dressed and rushed over to the couple's home only to find the young woman lying lifeless in her bed and the young husband sobbing inconsolably at her side.

After a long time of prying and pleading, the story was finally uncovered. Some weeks earlier this young woman had discovered that she was pregnant. With years of study still ahead, neither of them had wanted to start a family so soon. This sudden turn of events unsettled all their plans, driving them desperately in search of a solution. They considered every option. Finally, words escaped her lips that she had never dreamed she would utter. "This is completely devastating," she said. "There is no other way but to abort this child if our careers are to survive."

The very suggestion opened a deep rift between them. They were both known on campus for their outspoken conviction of the sanctity of the child's life in the womb. They fervently believed that each unborn child had a right all its own. Now, circumstances beyond their control had invaded their absolutes; "fate" had threatened their autonomy. Conviction clashed with ambition, and they agonized over a private decision they hoped would never be betrayed in public.

That is when she proposed her final solution. "Let's do this at home," she said. "You bring all the equipment we need to the apartment, and no one need ever know." As a young medical student, he felt this could be accomplished, and so they nervously laid meticulous plans for that fateful night. The young man was not yet fully trained in the administration of an anesthetic, and as he stumbled through the procedure he unwittingly gave her a much larger dose than he should have. His greatest fear became a ghastly deed, and he lost her. In the panicky moments that followed, with trembling hands and a cry of desperation, he reached for the telephone and uttered those remorse-ridden words, "Pastor, please hurry and come to our apartment. I think I've killed her!"[105]

They "considered every option." Did they? They were intent on no one ever knowing. This couple was part of a dedicated Christian fellowship with strong pro-life beliefs. The outcome would have been very different had they confessed their pain, confusion and devastation, having found out they were pregnant. Had they been brave enough to state that they, in desperation, were considering abortion because they didn't know what else to do, their friends would have rallied around them. Their friends would have helped them to a far better outcome and remained close to them to support them. Accountability is a powerful tool because secrets are banished. Secrets are both powerful and have a life of their own.

Guardrails

Think about the guardrail along a highway beside a precipice. Where, in relation to the drop off, is the guardrail placed? Usually the guardrail is three to four feet from the edge, not right on the precipice. Why? Because if a car hits the rail it will slow the car, hopefully preventing it from heading off the cliff. The barrier significantly reduces the momentum of the car before disaster happens. In addressing guardrails with our youth, we are asking them to think about setting their physical "guardrails" far enough from intercourse that, if they go beyond their rail, they will stop, realize where they are headed, and climb back behind their boundary. If they find they are often moving beyond this guardrail (overstepping their limit), they would do well to think about setting their rail farther from the precipice to prevent a weakening of their resolve.

Encourage your teens to use the Continuum of Sexual Arousal chart as they determine their own guardrails. Remind them that at times their guardrail will need to be adjusted because of particularly strong feelings. A friend used this image: "Set your guardrails in play dough not in concrete." For example, a woman's sexual feelings will be strongest when she is ovulating—the time when the body is designed to get egg and sperm connected. On such days, a woman needs to let her boyfriend know that her guardrail is temporarily moving to the left. On some days a man may know that he shouldn't be physically near his girlfriend because his feelings are too strong. In other words, guardrails need to be moveable; one placement does not fit all occasions. Communicating about this assures a boy/girlfriend that a "guardrail" move is not because of a cooling relationship but because of safety and respect.

Law of Diminishing Returns

Dawson McAlister explains this as "the law of diminishing returns, plus time alone, leads to disaster."[106] This is what he means: Think back to the first time you held your husband's/wife's hand. You had known each other for a time, maybe a long time. Maybe your relationship had grown slowly from a friendship into a romantic interest. One day, you were walking next to each other and the outside of your hands brushed against each other. Oh! What Joy! What rapture! "He/she touched me!" But it doesn't take long before the joy and rapture diminishes. Then, one day, he actually takes your hand. Wow! Once again the joy is back, the rapture, the thrill of the connection. Before long, however, you're walking together and almost automatically hold hands—no longer earth shaking, just a closeness. And now you start to think, What would it be like to hug or, better yet, to kiss him/her"? That would be it, you think, nothing more needed, I just want to kiss. If the relationship continues to develop on the physical plane, before too long the thrill, even of kissing, is gone or at least greatly diminished, and one desires more.

> **"The law of diminishing returns, plus time alone, leads to disaster."**

"Your hormones," says Dawson McAlister, "don't know that you're not married"[107] and the natural progression is toward more and more physicality until full intercourse results. One's natural desire is to push on to the next activity in the continuum until full intercourse and satisfaction. Without strong discipline the diminishing return from each activity can push a couple beyond their guardrails and off the cliff. Therefore, the ones who want to preserve their virginity will think carefully about this progression and purposefully set their guardrails, or physical activity line, at a place where each one can reasonably, comfortably tame their desire. Don't kid yourself by thinking you can handle this and just want to see how it feels. With each progression the feelings and desire get stronger and stronger until they are almost overpowering, while one's ability to resist gets weaker and weaker.

Suggestions For Parents and Teens

The old adage "an ounce of prevention is worth a pound of cure" holds true as you and your teens proactively establish ground rules regarding dating. Parents will help their teens if they:

➤ Discourage early, single dating.

➤ Encourage activities at church, at your home, or at the homes of trusted families.

➤ Know where your kids are (the 4 W's: What...Where...When...with Whom).

➤ Discourage hanging out without planned activities or adequate supervision (down time).

➤ Know what your kids are watching, reading and listening to (especially on the Internet).

➤ Keep checking in with them: "How's it going...?"

➤ Brain storm creative dating ideas. Dating can get pretty boring just doing the same things. See Appendix: Creative Dating Ideas. Use these ideas to stimulate your own.

The following are seven specific principles that it would be helpful to go over with your teens. Bear in mind that some of these principles are age-specific. For example, a 14-year-old may think she is old enough to trust her own ability to start down the physical continuum and be responsible. *You* need to discern whether or not she is. If your teens can commit to adhering to these principles, they'll be building helpful guardrails into their dating lives.

1. Don't do anything with a boy/girlfriend that you wouldn't do in front of your parents.

    Sam and Judy were nearly engaged to be married. They were alone in the living room of his home. Sam's mother needed a book that was in the living room. As she entered the room, Sam and Judy were sitting next to each other, arms around each other, and they didn't move a muscle. Sam's mom spoke briefly with them, got what she came for, and left the room. Later she commented to Sam:

"Do you know why I don't worry about you two: what you're doing when you're alone?

"No, why?"

"Because neither of you moved a muscle when I walked into the room."

2. Don't adopt an exclusive stance when talking with another, particularly a boy/girlfriend.

In an exclusive stance the couple demonstrates by their body language that no one else is welcome, even in a public place. For example, at school: the couple meet in the hall, stand close to each other face-to-face, and talk very quietly focusing only on one another. This definitely gives the message 'don't even think about approaching us.'

In a nonexclusive stance the couple demonstrates by their body language their interest in what's going on around them and welcomes others to interact with them. In the hallway at school, a couple meet, stand near each other but make eye contact with others, smiling, and welcoming others to come talk.

3. Choose group activities until well into a mature relationship.

4. Avoid single dating until after a well-established, mature relationship is in place.

5. Don't start down the physical continuum *at all* until each person can trust the other (they have discussed their respective guardrails and know they will each uphold and protect established boundaries).

6. Don't lie down next to each other.

7. Keep your clothes on.

The rewards for staying close with your high school youth are great. High school is an exciting time for them. With guidance and encouragement they go from irresponsible teens to young adults ready to go off into the world, ready for a great deal more independence, ready to leave the nest and ready to spread their wings. *Be part of this time with them!* It is far too exciting a time to be uninvolved and allow others to enjoy your child's blossoming. As they show signs of maturity, back off your monitoring of them and enjoy them as interesting young adults. Enjoy the fruit of your labor.

As the high school years draw to a close and your young person begins to think about what's after high school, make sure to talk with your son/daughter about what they are apt to face as they leave home. Your role in the years ahead may be less hands-on, but your wisdom and occasional guidance will still be helpful for your adult child. And, as you get older, you may find yourself turning to your children for their advice.

Chapter 11

POST HIGH SCHOOL YEARS

Three Pairs of Feet

Three pairs of feet, standing as we pray

Anticipate that they must walk away

These hands I hold have rocked me to sleep

And they've held me through the tough times,

when I just had to weep

These eyes that see me now have seen me grow

But now I know these eyes must see me go

Chorus:

But peace is found in knowing we are held in One hand

And joy is found in trusting One who understands

The years we shared must now be in the past

And looking back, I see them go so fast

I'll pray for you, and know you'll pray for me

And we will place all our hope in God's eternity

(David Jones, used by permission)

As your son/daughter leaves for college, they may be leaving an environment with clear boundaries and expectations and facing an environment with no boundaries and, other than academic work, few expectations. They could find themselves in a dorm with no structure—common bathrooms for men and women and co-ed suites, although an option is usually offered for students who desire more traditional living situations. Particularly in secular colleges, your child will be faced with sexual promiscuity and a whole lot of drinking and partying, with little to no importance put on faith and worship. Many students who have not been prepared for these aspects of college life don't know how to handle their newfound independence or living situations with no boundaries.

Loneliness

At a youth symposium entitled "Will Your Kids have Faith After High School?,"[108] Dr. Cheryl Crawford presented research showing that the biggest issue freshmen face is often completely unexpected: loneliness. Seniors in high school are usually frenetically busy and programmed to the max. They have lots of friends and acquaintances; they excitedly anticipate getting away from home and being on their own; but they are totally unprepared for the sense of loneliness they will face and the large amounts of unstructured time.

Jane couldn't wait to get to college. The thought of finally being away and independent was exhilarating. The thought of the freedom that college affords sustained her during her senior year and the summer following. Finally, it was time. But as she got closer and closer to the college, her stomach grew more and more queasy. Could it be anxiety? No—she had been looking forward to this for the past year at least. They arrived. Her parents helped her unpack her belongings, move into her room, and meet her new roommate, a stranger in a dorm full of strangers. Her parents then kissed her goodbye and left. Jane stood on the corner and waved them off, watching their car until it turned the corner at the end of the block. Standing outside of her new home (her freshman dorm), she was hit with an incredibly strong, totally unexpected loneliness unlike anything she had ever experienced before. It was physical. She felt as if she had hit a wall. She wept, feeling utterly depressed, then wandered off alone, trying desperately to get herself together. How was she going to face her roommate and the others who seemed to have it all together? Every time she thought she could handle her feelings, something reminded her of home and she'd weep. This continued until she formed relationships and made new friends.

Sean's loneliness didn't hit until going back to college after Christmas vacation. After the warm, comfortable, familiar time he returned to a place where he still felt somewhat a stranger. He called his parents soon after returning to school, deeply homesick and not knowing how he was going to manage. Suddenly, a fire alarm sounded and he had to go. About an hour later he called back saying that the fire drill was a blessing: he got outside his dorm and was surrounded by many friends who boosted his spirits. His emotions settled and that was the end of his homesickness.

Talk to your soon-to-be college students about how they will face any periods of loneliness they may encounter. Help them think through some strategies for dealing with this. When they get to college, be available to take their phone calls. Encourage them to call when they are lonely, facing a significant decision, or about to take a difficult exam. Usually it is best if they call you. If you call them, they may be too busy or not want to talk; but when they call you, they *need* to talk!

Alcohol and Sex on Campus

Dr. Crawford found that students who were not prepared with strategies for dealing with loneliness were ripe for an invitation to college parties. These parties often open the door to drinking, as a way of dealing with loneliness, as well as sexual involvement. At that point, students' lives could tragically jump to an unexpected track.

Alcohol use is huge on most campuses. When asked what surprised her most in her research with college students, Dr. Crawford responded, "the amount of alcohol consumption."[109] She adds: "Available research indicates that about 80% of college students drink, and half of those engage in heavy episodic drinking."[110] Excessive consumption of alcohol can results in injury, death, and long-term problems for the drinker and 'innocent' others. Forty-eight percent of all alcohol use reported by college students occurs among those who are underage.[111]

The link between alcohol consumption and sex is well documented:

➢ An American Medical Association (AMA) fact sheet states that "Alcohol is a major contributing factor in sexual activity among youth."[112]

➢ "Alcohol abuse is linked to as many as 2/3 of all sexual assaults and date rapes of teens and college students..."[113]

> ➤ Thirty-two percent of girls ages 17-18 said that drugs or alcohol had influenced their decision to have sex. Without being under the influence they would not have succumbed to sexual pressure.[114]

> ➤ Research has shown a strong association between alcohol use and multiple sexual partners.[115]

Before your children leave for college, help them think through how they will handle party invitations where the point is to drink until drunk. How will they handle the amount of sex they will become aware of? And, if they choose to walk a different path, how will they handle being different?

World View and Faith

Dr. Crawford stated that at secular colleges, if students do not connect to a church or campus ministry within two weeks of coming to campus as freshmen, they are apt to lose their faith or put it on a shelf where it may remain for at least ten years.[116] Parents or youth leaders may need to help their students connect. Parents, before you take your high school students to potential colleges, research not only the academic aspects of the college but also the campus ministries available. Plan to visit with the leadership of these ministries. Get a feeling for the support these ministries offer. Research, ahead of time, the churches near the campus. Contact those churches; ask for someone you can visit with and connect your student to. Once your student chooses a college, be certain that someone from a church or campus ministry will welcome him to campus, take him to ministry gatherings, see that he gets connected with others, and have a means of transportation available, if needed.

Dr. J.J. Arnett, research professor in the Department of Psychology at Clark University, identifies the following three areas of adolescent identity necessary to move into adulthood: worldview, work and love.[117] If your student leaves home with a pretty solid worldview, the other two—work and love—will follow in time. Worldview is defined as "the overall perspective from which one sees and interprets the world; a collection of beliefs about life and the universe held by an individual or a group."[118] As she is ready to leave for college, does your student own her own faith or is her faith more a hand-me-down from you? Does she have a reasonable ability to articulate why she believes as she does about who God is and who she is? If she leaves home with that aspect of her life firmly in place and a determination to continue in fellowship with other believers, then, although she will face struggles, she will have a group of trusted friends and older, wiser people who will help her in her trials, hold her accountable for her behavior, and encourage her to take on adult responsibility. She will not, like many of her classmates, just be wandering, forever seeking. Encourage her to walk the narrow way: "For the gate is wide and the way is easy that leads to destruction, and those who enter by it are many. For the gate is narrow and the way is hard that leads to life, and those who find it are few" (Matthew 7:13b-14).

Gap Year

By the time your child is in his or her last years of high school, you know him or her well. How far along are they with the task of identity definition? If they need more time in this endeavor it may be wise to consider a gap year with a focus. The following testimony illustrates the value of a gap year for one young man.

> I was helping to lead a five-day backpacking training program for some of the new staff at the camp. All of the guys in the group were either my age or older. Every morning, I had been doing a Bible study for the guys. Most of the guys in this group came from hard backgrounds. No one in the group had a problem with anyone else but they never shared about themselves and hardly even talked to each other. Their pride and hurt from the past was too great for them to be able to be vulnerable with each other and this was keeping them from growing in Christ as a group. It was really a sad thing to see. On the last morning we studied the story of Jesus' washing his disciples' feet, after which we proceeded to wash each other's feet. Something about seeing myself and the others serve each other in that manner broke down some of the walls those guys had. Some were crying and all opened up to each other and worshiped Jesus together. It was amazing to see and I thank God that I could be a part of such an experience of the freedom Christ brings.[119]

A gap year can be just what is needed for some.

In the past several chapters we have looked at topics that need to be addressed as children grow. Hopefully, you find that in nurturing a close relationship with your children they are talking. If, however, you find your teens have erected a barrier of silence, because you started talking relatively late in their development or because they are quiet by nature, don't give up! Keep looking for ways to improve communication.

Chapter 12

PROACTIVE NOT REACTIVE

Don't wait for your children to ask, talk to them at every stage of their development. If you wait for them to ask, they won't, because they will get the point that the subject of sex is not something you want to discuss. Once again, talking early and often sets the stage for further conversations and eventually gives you the platform upon which to talk to them about the purpose for sex.

Understand enough about the physical, emotional and intellectual development of children to prepare them for their changing bodies, emotions and behavior. For example, you want to be preparing them for pubescent changes as much as two years before the change begins to happen. This gives them time to adjust to what's coming as well as lots of time for them to get their questions answered and receive assurance. Pubescent body changes can be unsettling for some children, so offer lots of assurance before, during and after the changes. Anticipate what's ahead for your children both physically and emotionally and talk about things that will come up *before* they happen. For example, consider dating. Before they are interested in dating, think through and discuss what wise and appropriate boundaries will look like. This goes for all of the issues they will face. Try to anticipate as many as you can and talk about them. In this way your child will not be taken by surprise and you won't have to suddenly deal with issues you are unprepared for.

Take time to discuss issues with your spouse before trying to guide your children, so that you will be on the same page. It is much easier when parents' perspective on issues of child rearing are in agreement. When parents disagree, as you may well know, children can use such disagreements to pit one parent against the other, not necessarily to be manipulative, but as a way of getting what they want. Try to present a unified front, if at all possible.

Family Rules

You probably won't think of all the issues that need to be discussed as your children enter adolescence. Nevertheless, by having early discussions on difficult issues both parent and adolescent develop a pattern that can be followed in subsequent years. Establish things like: both parents need to agree; agreement needs to be reached before an activity; discussion takes place face-to-face; discussion needs to happen in private, not on the phone or with friends around.

At what age will you allow dating? Establish this in advance. When they do start dating, emphasize that they will need to provide you with their date's cell phone number (if he/she has one) as well as phone numbers for their date's parents. Emphasize this is for safety purposes, so you can contact them if necessary.

Address the driving issues. When can they use the car? Who will they be able to drive? Who pays for gas and the increased car insurance? Having them share a family car, replace gas used, and pay for the increased insurance both reminds them that growing up involves responsibilities and short-circuits thoughts of entitlement. It helps enormously to have this understood before they are ready to drive.

One young man, as he approached driving age, knew he would be responsible for paying the increased cost of car insurance. When he thought of all the things he could do with that money, he decided to postpone getting his license.

What are your family rules regarding your children and their friends? Where can they hang out—at the mall, at other people's homes? How much supervision do you expect at other people's homes? What are the guidelines when they go to the home of a boy/girlfriend? When they bring a friend of the opposite sex to your home, talk about what rooms are acceptable for them to be in: family areas and not bedrooms.

John was good friends with Susan. Their parents were also good friends. John was at Susan's home one evening with her family when he needed to make a phone call and Susan told him to use the phone in her bedroom. He followed her to her bedroom only to have Susan's father very severely admonish him for being in her room.

It would have avoided embarrassment had Susan's parents emphasized that never should a member of the opposite sex be in her bedroom for any reason.

What do you consider appropriate clothing, particularly for girls? ("But, Mom, everyone is wearing this!") What curfews, including bedtimes,

135

should they expect? Where does homework fit into activities and social engagements?

Don't wait for a behavior to happen before talking about it. Parents are often taken by surprise when their children seem to suddenly grow up. Seemingly out of the blue a preadolescent is on the phone, hand over the mouth piece, begging her mom: "Please, please, please let me go to the mall this afternoon with my friends. Everyone is going, and if you don't let me, I'll be the only one!" This puts inordinate pressure on a parent to decide, on the spot, whether or not this is wise. Furthermore, parents have no time to discuss the appropriateness of the given activity. Have the child hang up while you discuss the matter, then phone them back with the answer.

The above relies on talking, both parent(s) and teen. But what if your teen mumbles one-word answers...or nothing at all?

My Teen Won't Talk—"Silent" Acrostic

"But you don't know my child," you say. "Talking to him is like talking to a brick wall." What do we do if our teens won't talk, if they are silent? This is indeed hard, but don't give up. Seek ways to further relationship by finding things that interest them. Search for times to engage your child even though they may seem unresponsive. Keep praying for wisdom and insight; keep praying for them.

A good friend whose husband left her tells of raising her two sons. She felt as if she had very few common interests with them. The boys' greatest interest was sports, a subject she was not the least bit interested in and knew very little about. So, she set about informing herself about the sports they liked—asking them questions, watching games on TV, going to games with them—and in that way she deepened her relationship with them.

Another friend tells of his struggle to emotionally reach his adoptive daughter. She had lost both her parents at an early age and finally been adopted in early adolescence. He said that after she became a part of their family, he'd drive her to school every day. As she got out of the car he would wish her a good day and add, "I love you." And every day his daughter would walk away with no reply. This went on for approximately 173 days, eight months, until one day after his "I love you" his daughter turned to him and responded, "I love you too, Dad."

The following acrostic on the word "silent" gives some thoughts and suggestions which might be helpful:

S - Share your own experience in adolescence.

   I - Inventory means to good communication. Build on these.

      L - Learn from stories and writing.

         E - Engage feelings: "How do you feel about ___?"

            N - Needed: You must be open and honest yourself.

            T - Time: Are you available?

Let's consider these thoughts and suggestions one-by-one.

Share your own experience in adolescence. Kids easily forget that parents were adolescents once. Sometimes they will open up when we are willing to share some of our own experiences, including funny stories, stories of adventure, and crazy things we did. They will often respond with questions about the stories, opening up as a result of the dialogue.

One set of parents told about the many, many letters they had written each other while they were dating. They intrigued their listening youth when they told how they wrote secret messages under the stamp: the recipient had to either steam off the stamp or carefully peel it away to get the message. They even pulled out their love letters and read some of the messages.

Inventory means to good communication. What are some things that you and your teen enjoy doing together? Do moms and daughters take pleasure in shopping or going out for tea? Do dads and sons enjoy working on cars together or building things? Doing puzzles together? Hiking together? During shared activities like these, try to open up conversations where, in this safe environment, your teen may talk.

Learn from stories and writing. Use any kind of media that might prompt comment from your teen. Focusing on someone else's story is much easier than focusing on your teen's situation. It is much easier to ask questions about behavior if it isn't their behavior. "What do you think about the way that person acted?" (Use a character from the story as the focus of discussion.)

One family found it helpful to communicate about difficult issues in writing. They had a 'Communication Notebook.' When either parent or youth had a question or comment, the question or comment was to be written in the notebook. The notebook would be left on the bed of the one who was to respond. Within a day's time the answer or comment needed to be submitted and the notebook returned.

Another family fell upon a marvelous means of communication through a tooth fairy envelope. This started when their child was young and continued into adolescence—way beyond belief in the tooth fairy. It started with the first lost tooth that was carefully placed in an envelope under the pillow of the six-year-old. This small boy also enclosed a letter to the tooth fairy. The next day, the envelope was still under his pillow. The boy was distressed thinking the tooth fairy had forgotten him until he felt the envelope—no tooth. When he opened it, he found a return note from the tooth fairy. This back and forth continued throughout the lost teeth phase, then morphed into a means of questions and answers of a more personal nature, even into questions about the opposite sex and dating. Of course, by that time, the boy/teen knew that he was communicating with one of his parents and not a tooth fairy.

One-on-one in the car is a good place to encourage teens to talk. Don't allow distractions. Turn off the radio; discourage ear phones plugged into whatever device (which essentially block you out); just be together, the two of you, in the car. You are both captive with nothing to do but listen and talk. This might be a good practice even if you have no particular issue that you want to address. You might think about using car rides as communication times. From the time your children are little, practice talking in the car, not listening to the radio or talking on the phone. *Make car rides and meal times communication times.*

If you have something you want to talk about, bring it up and leave it. Don't try to answer for them; try to be comfortable in the silence and wait. If they refuse to talk, at the end of the journey remind them that you really want to talk about the issue and ask him/her to think about the question. Get back to it later, maybe when in the car again. Not being face-to-face makes difficult communication much easier. (Taking a hike together provides the same comfortable distance).

Engage feelings. This can be done either with verbal or written communication. The point here is to get your teen thinking about how he/she is reacting to changes in his body, both physical and emotional. If your teen will engage with you in this or a similar activity, it will lend further help in cementing a close, trusting, intimate relationship. By sharing feelings we draw closer to one another.

Need to be honest. The more open, honest, and transparent you are about yourself, the more your teen will be willing to share with you. Make this a policy from their earliest years. (See Section Four: "Getting Personal: Being Real and Honest.")

And, of course, all of the above require *Time*. Kids seem to have a talent for picking the most inconvenient times to want to talk. For example, just when you are about to fall asleep you may get a knock on the door and a loaded question: "Mom/Dad, How do you know if a girl really likes you?" Wake up, get your thinking cap on, and engage them in conversation. Question them to be certain you understand exactly what it is they want to talk about, then get them to express themselves before you give advice. Talking, building relationship, and communication take time.

Setting and Holding to Boundaries

One of the tasks of fallen humanity seems to be to test limits. Look again at our beginning. God said you can eat of any tree in the garden except the tree of the knowledge of good and evil. So, what did they want to eat? The fruit from the *one* forbidden tree. Adam and Eve tested that boundary with catastrophic consequences.

In testing boundaries, however, we are often also looking for, and even hoping for, restraints. So, parents, don't be fooled by your teen's frequent pushing against boundaries. Hold fast to what you know is good for them.

Patsy Lowell tells this story with a rather surprising ending:

When our second daughter, Kathleen, was 13, she was as lively as any young teenager could be. One night, she excitedly asked permission to buy a leather miniskirt, one like all the other girls in her class were wearing.

As she described the benefits, I could tell she was expecting a negative response. Nonetheless, she acted surprised when I said no.

Kathleen then launched into great detail about how she would be the only one in the class without a leather miniskirt. I reminded her that my answer was no and explained my reasons.

"Well, I think you're wrong!" She retorted.

"Wrong or right, I've made the decision. The answer is no."

Kathleen stomped off, but quickly turned on her heels.

"I just want to explain why this is so important to me."

I nodded.

"If I don't have this miniskirt, I'll be left out, and all my friends won't like me."

"The answer is no," I quietly repeated.

She puffed up like a balloon and played her final card.

"I thought you loved me," she wailed.

"I do. But the answer is still no."

With that, she "whumped"—a noise made only by an angry junior high kid trying to get her way. She ran upstairs and slammed her bedroom door....

The whumping noise from Kathleen's bedroom started once more, and sure enough, she appeared on the stairwell. This time, she was breathing fire.

"I thought you taught us that we have rights!" she screamed.

"You do have rights. The answer is still no."

She wound up again, but I cut her off. "Kathleen, I have made my decision. I will not change my mind, and if you say another word about this, you will be severely punished. Now go to bed!"

She still had a few words left, but she held them in check. She loped off to bed, still seething....

Just when I thought our skirmishes were over, the sound of whumping came again. Kathleen came down the stairs.

"Well," she announced, "I'm just going to tell you one more time...."

I met her at the bottom step, planted my hands on my hips and looked her in the eyes.

"Do not answer," I said. "Do not say yes or no. Do not say anything. Do not say 'Yes, ma'am' or 'No, ma'am.' Turn around and go to bed. And do not make a single sound!"

She slowly turned and trudged upstairs without a word. I dropped onto the couch, thoroughly exhausted....Then I heard her door open. Kathleen, her nose and eyes red from crying, walked down the stairs in pajamas. Curlers were in her hair. She held out her hands to me.

"Oh, Mom, I'm sorry."

We hugged as she said through her tears, "I was so scared!"

"Scared of what?"

"I was scared that you were going to let me win!" she sniffled....[120]

Deep down, teens know they need guidance and leadership. That's why they often come back to thank us. Parents, it's up to us to give and hold to what we know they need.

External to Internal Monitoring

As teens grow older, encourage them to move from external monitoring to internal monitoring. When parents have young children in a house with stairs, they usually have child gates (external monitor) at the top of their stairs. When they are a bit older, they no longer need this monitor. The gates come down because children learn to safely negotiate stairs (internal monitoring). "Internet Nannies" and blocks on computers are helpful when young people are beginning to use the Internet by themselves. Again, these are external monitors and helpful for a time. As teens get older, if they are focused on being rebellious, they can figure ways around blocking devices. Nevertheless, the hope is that they will move from external monitoring to internal monitoring. As you observe them, you will be able to tell if this transfer is taking place. As you see that they have incorporated internal monitors you can then trust them to follow the path they know is right, and you can back off. It is important that both parents and teens understand that trust is earned; it is not a given and cannot be demanded by our children. With every new behavior or activity that teens embark upon, they need to demonstrate to their parents that they are capable of handling the new activity.

Ginny and Bill didn't want to be overprotective parents. They were convinced that when their kids looked like adults, they were adults. And when, for example, their kids got their driver's license, they believed they were ready to take on the responsibility of driving, no matter the extenuating circumstances. Rather than giving driving privileges according to demonstrated abilities and responsible decisions, they turned the family car over to their teens almost whenever they wanted to use it, no questions asked. One day, Craig, their 17-year-old son, wanted to take the car for a Saturday activity. He had had little driving experience on muddy roads, but he had a license to drive so the car was turned over to him. One has to experience the fifth season, "Mud Season," in Vermont to know what it can be like on unpaved roads. The mud on these roads gets so deep that one year a huge road grader got buried in mud as the operator tried to grade a particularly bad section of road. The day Craig asked for the car turned out to be in the midst of a particularly bad "Mud Season" when the roads were treacherous. Bill and Ginny hadn't asked when Craig expected to be home, nor had they asked where he was going or if he'd be driving others, but they assumed he'd be back for dinner since he left in the late morning. Dinner time came and went, the evening wore on, and still no Craig. Finally, around 11:00 p.m., Bill and Ginny's anxiety level had reached the breaking point. They took another car and began searching for their son. They had little to go on since they had not asked where he expected to be throughout the day. Finally, around 1 a.m., they got a call saying that their son and his friend had been found. They had been driving on extremely muddy roads when the car got stuck in a deep rut and slid off into a ditch in a remote area with no cell phone coverage. It was quite spring-like when they left that Saturday morning, so they had dressed in light jackets only. They had no boots to navigate the deep mud, so when they got stranded they had no ability to walk anywhere. The temperature had precipitously dropped while they were waiting for someone to pass. Without the sleeping bags stowed in the back of the car they would have had significant problems with the cold. Mercifully, someone finally passed and promised to get help to them.

How can a parent trust one who acted as Craig did? Trust needs to be earned not just assumed because of a given age. To drive into very difficult conditions with no training, to go off in the spring into the remote country with clothing not suitable for changeable weather, to go off without heavy boots to navigate mud and not to share anything about his plans, do not make for the ingredients of trust. Mature thinking, planning and practice needs to be demonstrated before a parent should trust their young person. A wise parent expects their sons and daughters to earn trust by demonstrating capability and responsible thinking before more independence is given. Frequently young people, when denied permission for a given activity, will respond, "Don't you trust me?"

A very appropriate answer from a parent is, "How can I trust you? You've never done this before."

Trust is not a given; it needs to be demonstrated, and thus earned.

In building trust, try having conversations with teens where various scenarios are posed and talked about. Ask questions such as, "What would you do if (such and such happens)?"

Give various scenarios and ask them how they'd handle the situation: "You're riding with a friend to a party. Your friend drinks too much and you feel he's not safe for the return drive, but he won't turn the car over to you. What would you do?"

"How would you respond if you were at a friend's home and your friend tried to show you a pornographic movie?"

"Your date took you out for a really nice dinner then, despite your objections, took you back to his apartment. What would you do?"

These, or other scenarios you come up with, are helpful to talk through with your teen(s). Discuss the best response for each situation. Such dialogue will prompt good thinking and serve as a way for teens to plan how to act and consider the possible consequences if they remain passive. Involve the whole family in such exchanges. These exercises can be likened to fire drills: practicing behavior. As you hear thoughtful, responsible answers you can be more confident in their maturity which, in turn, helps greatly in building your trust in them.

Is It Proactive or Reactive Parenting?

Reactive parenting is characterized by rules (don't...) and legalism. However, as Josh McDowell wisely points out: "rules without relationship lead to rebellion."[121] "Legalism," states Jerram Barrs, "fosters rebellion against parents, schools, and churches, and ultimately against God."[122]

Rules are necessary when children are young, and external monitoring is the way we all learn. In the enforcement of these rules and the presence of consistent boundaries, parents build trust and relationships with their children. As children become adolescents, monitoring should become more and more internal. Parents should be able to place less and less emphasis on external rules and, instead, listen, question and advise.

Proactive parenting helps kids understand what's good, healthy and acceptable. It includes much interaction: talking through issues, a lot of active listening, reasonable boundaries set and enforced (boundaries that make sense to both teen and parent). All of this prepares teens to make their own good and wise decisions in the future.

"Rules without relationship lead to rebellion."

From pre-school through high school you are trying to enlighten and prepare your children for changes in their physical and emotional selves, steer them away from harmful influences and set them on a healthy course as they head into their adult years. *So, talk with them.* Rather than waiting for change, prepare them. Model through conversation and behavior how to be proactive in life and not reactive.

Hearing God's Call

Chapter 13

GOD'S CALL FOR COMMUNICATION

"There is a way that seems right to a man, but its end is the way to death." (Proverbs 14:12)

Is the way of the majority necessarily right? Who are we to guide our children in a counter-cultural direction?

How often do our children try to lobby us by arguing, "But Mom/Dad, everyone is going! If you don't let me go (or have that), I'll be the only one...." In the sexual realm, we are barraged by our culture's messages that sex before marriage is actually good for us. To suppress one's natural desire is not good; it can do great damage, we're told.

"Hardly anyone today would deny that in the modern West, the prevailing cultural mood is one of moral relativism. A majority of people in the United States, for example, would deny that there is any absolute truth, especially when it comes to matters of personal and private behavior...."[123]

A confusion of the terms morals and ethics lies at the heart of moral relativism. Ethics has traditionally been seen as that which addresses the way things ought to be. We have been made by a Creator and He has stated what our behavior should be in order for us to be healthy in every sense of the word.

Morals, historically, have been considered a descriptive science looking at what people are actually doing: looking at what *is* rather than looking at what ought to be. Too often, parents believe that what the majority (or near majority) is doing must be right and, therefore, there is no need to talk with their children about sex because they are going to do what everyone else is doing anyway. They'll just do what comes naturally.

We all need to be reminded, constantly, of the truth of how we are made and how our Creator calls us to act. This constant reminder counters and combats the powerful force and constant barrage of media, our contemporaries, and even some in authority.

Parents Are Commanded to Talk

Many parents are unaware that God calls them to talk to their children about sex. The clarion call in Deuteronomy 6:4-6 is to revisit His directives and apply them to our daily lives, to talk often about everything in God's creation: "You shall teach them diligently to your sons and shall talk of them when you sit in your house and when you walk by the way and when you lie down and when you rise up" (Deuteronomy 6:7, NASB).

The "talk of them" refers to God's commandments. God calls us to do a whole lot of talking and the subject matter includes the way He made us and how He designed His good gift of sex to be used.

Does anyone hold their newborn baby in their arms and dream about the future of that child, visualizing sexually transmitted diseases, promiscuous sexual relations, broken hearts, and broken homes? Do we want them to go the way of the world, or do we want for them to have a good possibility of living happy, healthy, fulfilled lives? If left to themselves, they are apt to go the way of the world. Parents, consciously or unconsciously, choose to guide their children using the wisdom of humanity or the wisdom of God. Choosing to guide children by the wisdom of humanity often entails simply leaving their education to peers and media. Encouraging children to follow God's way means teaching them about God and how He has instructed us to live, and thus leads them toward the way of abundant life.

How often are parents to talk to their children about God? As Deuteronomy 6 tells us, "when you sit in your house, and when you walk by the way, and when you lie down, and when you rise"—essentially, all day long.

How often in a day do we hear our culture's view of life? We see and hear it in advertising. We're likely to see it in movies and in television programs. What we have in front of us, what we hear all the time, is what we are apt to believe. Why is so much spent on advertising? Keep the product in front of people and they will believe that:

"You deserve a break today."

"_____, the choice of a new generation..."

"...probably the best beer in the world."

"Quality never goes out of style."

"Just do it."

"Come to where the flavor is."

"The best part of waking up is _____ in your cup."

"There are some things money can't buy. For everything else, there's _____."

"Don't leave home without it."

We hear such advertisements again and again until they are ingrained in our thinking, and when it comes time to choose among many possibilities, we often believe what has been drilled into our heads.

A nurse who was pregnant with her first child spent part of every day of her pregnancy in the Newborn Intensive Care Nursery. Day after day she saw tiny, premature infants weighing less than four pounds. Although she knew in her head that her baby was growing toward normal newborn weight, what she saw every day was an entire population of severely underweight babies. It was not until after her baby was born that she realized she had been expecting her baby to look just like the babies she had seen every day of her pregnancy.

God wants parents to keep Him and His truth front and center in the thinking of their children. That is why He calls us to talk about Him all the time.

Societal Consensus Before and After the 1960s

It used to be agreed that sex was to be saved until marriage. The National Opinion Research Center (NORC) has conducted yearly nationwide surveys since 1972. One of the questions asked is: "If a man and woman have sex relations before marriage, do you think it is always wrong, almost always wrong, wrong only sometimes, or not wrong at all?"

GOD'S CALL FOR COMMUNICATION

In 1972, 26% responded "not wrong at all" and

34.9% responded "always wrong."
In 2010, 51.8% responded "not wrong at all" and
20.8% responded "always wrong."[124]

It used to be that society expected youth to 'be good,' to 'remember your moral compass.' Now, the culture expects everyone to do what he or she wants—if it feels good, do it. Good is defined by each person deciding what he or she thinks is right for them. Unfortunately, consequences are rarely considered.

Being pregnant out of wedlock used to be looked upon as shameful. Now, little if any stigma is attached to the condition. If you were sleeping with your boyfriend in the 1960s you didn't talk about it. Now, no one even blushes when talking about cohabitating. Even parents of cohabitating children talk about their kids "living together" with no hesitation, sadness or embarrassment. In some colleges in the 1960s and before, if you became pregnant out of wedlock anytime up to the day of graduation, you were dismissed from the college.

Joanne was in her senior year when she became pregnant. Knowing the university's no tolerance policy about unwed mothers, she went to great lengths to hide her increasing girth. She even fooled her friends who thought she was simply putting on weight. She delivered her baby a few weeks after graduating.

The institution's severe reaction in that era was pure legalism, lacking compassion. I use it to illustrate the huge contrast to the attitudes of today.

Fifty years ago, the following sequence was the accepted societal norm:

dating, engagement, marriage, sex, family. This was considered healthy sequencing. In today's culture, more typically the sequence is: dating, sex, maybe get pregnant, maybe engagement, maybe marriage, but maybe never marriage. Even some Christians are not aware of healthy sequencing because they've never been told; they have never understood the way God designed us to live.

Peter and Jane were devoted and active members of a Christian campus ministry. They came to Bible studies and other activities and participated in service projects sponsored by the ministry. They dated, fell in love, became sexually involved, then decided that, economically, it made sense to live together. They didn't hide their intent from the leaders of the Christian group; in fact, they were excited to share about the place they planned to rent, then about the fact that they had signed a lease and would shortly be moving in together.

One of the leaders, a winsome, thoughtful, sincere young man, was troubled by their decision. He wrestled long and hard about whether to talk to them about their decision to live together. After one long night of thinking and praying, this young man felt he needed to talk with them. He pointed out what the Bible teaches about sex and its place in our lives. When he finished with his gentle but thorough presentation, Peter and Jane were astounded. They said, with great passion, that no one had ever told them that before.

They proceeded to tear up their lease, resulting in some financial loss for both of them, and lived apart until they married. They remain grateful for the leader who loved them enough to point out God's truth.

The Bible Is Frank; Parents Should Be Too

Having established that God commands parents to talk frequently about His ways, what guidance is given as to how frankly one should talk about sex? Looking to the Bible as a guide, from Genesis right through Revelation, sex, marriage, divorce and family are plainly talked about. They are also used as metaphors to explain the depth of relationship God wants to have with His people: to awaken His bride, the church, to the yearning heart of her waiting groom, Jesus our Lord and Savior.

Here are a few examples of sex being plainly talked about in the early books of the Bible. Sex for procreation is cited in Genesis 4:1a (NLB): "Now Adam had sexual relations with his wife, Eve, and she became pregnant." In Genesis 19:5 (NIV), homosexual sex is mentioned: "They called to Lot, 'Where are the men who came to you tonight? Bring them out to us so that we can have sex with them.'" Reading through Leviticus 18, there is frank discussion about incest, menstrual periods and bestiality.

In the Song of Solomon one finds a frank discussion of the beauty of marital sex: "Behold, you are beautiful, my love, behold, you are beautiful! Your eyes...Your hair...Your teeth...Your lips...Your neck...Your two breasts are like two fawns, twins of a gazelle, that graze among the lilies" (excerpted from Song of Solomon 4). Ezekiel 16 describes female sexual development: "I made you flourish like a plant of the field. And you grew up and became tall and arrived at full adornment. Your breasts were formed, and your hair had grown; yet you were naked and bare" (Ezekiel 16:7). And Ezekiel 23 is a graphic description of lewd, adulterous behavior as a metaphor pointing out the idolatrous behavior of Israel and Judah:

'Yet she increased her whoring, remembering the days of her youth, when she played the whore in the land of Egypt and lusted after her paramours there, whose members were like those of donkeys, and whose issue was like that of horses.

Thus you longed for the lewdness of your youth, when the Egyptians handled your bosom and pressed your young breasts.' (Ezekiel 23:19-21)

Does God Want Children Hearing about Sex?

Parents are often concerned about the age at which children should hear about sex. Joshua 8:34-35 makes it clear that God intended that even children hear His instructions about life, including how sex is to be used:

And afterward he read all the words of the law, the blessings and the curse, according to all that is written in the Book of the Law. There was not a word of all that Moses commanded that Joshua did not read before all the assembly of Israel, and the women, and *the little ones*, and the sojourners who lived among them. (Joshua 8:34-35, emphasis added)

The Book of the Law, Genesis through Deuteronomy in the Bible, has much to say about sex and sexuality. Because 'little ones' assumes children younger than age twelve (the age of majority in Israel), parents should use their discernment, remembering to start early in simpler terms and progress with more specifics. The point is that sex is part of God-given life and, in parenting, we're required to talk about it.

Chapter 14

DOES THE BIBLE HAVE A SEXUAL ETHIC?

The Bible has much to say about sex throughout its pages. But does the Bible set out an 'oughtness' about sex? Does the Bible have a sexual ethic?

During the debate over civil unions in Vermont, someone claimed the Bible has no sexual ethic. After reading the biblical references in this next section, see if you agree with the above statement. Referring back to the earlier discussion on moral relativism, God's Word clearly tells us the way we ought to use sex. Furthermore, it tells us that if we honor His commandments, we will find peace and joy; if we don't, we will eventually find pain and suffering.

The morals of the culture—developed in America particularly after the 1960s—aren't working. They have led to much pain, alienation, family breakup and heartache. It's time to look back to the intentions of our good Creator and see what He had in mind when He gave the good, fun gift of sex. What does the Bible say about how sex is to be used?

Sex Is for Marriage

"For this reason a man will leave his father and mother and be united to his wife, and they will become one flesh" (Genesis 2:24, NIV).

Here, right at the beginning, we see God's intent for sex to take place within marriage. This passage immediately follows the description of how God made woman out of Adam's rib. Two separate and different creatures were brought together again *after their marriage* for the act of sexual union which would result in their becoming one flesh.

Matthew Henry comments on God making Eve from Adam's rib: "The woman was made of a rib out of the side of Adam; not made out of his head to rule over her, nor out of his feet to be trampled upon by him, but out of his side to be equal with him, under his arm to be protected, and near to his heart to be beloved."[125]

Sex: a Profound Intimacy

"Now Adam knew Eve his wife..." (Genesis 4:1a). Adam has sexual intercourse with his wife, Eve, but the word used in some translations is "to know." God intended sex to be a significant act, a profound intimacy which can only be fully experienced when sex is added to a loving, caring, life-long relationship. A relationship implies time and commitment, and marriage seals that committed relationship.

Sex Is for Procreation

"...and she conceived and bore Cain" (Genesis 4:1b). One of God's purposes for sex within marriage is to bring children into a family to be raised by their biological parents. Procreation is one of the verbs used to describe the making of offspring by reproduction. Pro Creation: pro can mean "in favor of" or "for." Sex is given to be used in marriage so a husband and wife can participate in creation—not as God created (from nothing), but to start new life.

Sex in Marriage Comforts

"Then Isaac brought her [Rebekah] into the tent of Sarah his mother and took Rebekah, and she became his wife, and he loved her. So Isaac was comforted after his mother's death" (Genesis 24:67).

Sex in Marriage Is for Pleasure and Enjoyment

"When Isaac had been there a long time, Abimelech king of the Philistines looked down from a window and saw Isaac caressing his wife Rebekah" (Genesis 26:8, NIV).

Throughout the Song of Solomon one reads about the beauty and enjoyment found in marital sex.

Sexual Obedience Leads to Fullness of Life

"You shall walk in all the way that the LORD your God has commanded you, that you may live, and that you may live long in the land that you shall possess" (Deuteronomy 5:33).

God calls us to obey Him, to live as He designed us to live. This is not because He is a dictator, nor just because He said so or because He rules over us, but because He made us, He loves us, and He knows how we work best. If we behave as He intended, we will live. We will be full, at peace, content and joyful.

Protecting, Caring and Cherishing

"'Who are you?' he asked. She answered, 'I am Ruth. Spread the corner of your garment over me because you are a close relative who can take care of me'" (Ruth 3:9, GW). And they married. This beautiful love story found in Scripture portrays the marriage union in terms of protecting, caring and cherishing.

Satisfaction and Contentment

"Let your fountain be blessed, and rejoice in the wife of your youth, a lovely deer, a graceful doe. Let her breasts fill you at all times with delight; be intoxicated always in her love" (Proverbs 5:18-19).

God's Good Gift in Marriage

"House and wealth are inherited from fathers, but a prudent wife is from the LORD" (Proverbs 19:14b). "An excellent wife who can find? She is far more precious than jewels" (Proverbs 31:10). And from Malachi: "Didn't the LORD make you one with your wife? In body and spirit you are his. And what does he want? Godly children from your union. So guard your heart; remain loyal to the wife of your youth" (Malachi 2:15, NLT).

Jesus on Marriage

"Therefore a man shall leave his father and his mother and hold fast to his wife, and the two shall become one flesh.... What therefore God has joined together, let not man separate" (Matthew 19:5, 6b). Jesus goes on to say that marriage, and therefore sex (because sex is for marriage only), is not for everyone:

But Jesus said, 'Not everyone is mature enough to live a married life. It requires a certain aptitude and grace. Marriage isn't for everyone. Some, from birth seemingly, never give marriage a thought. Others never get asked—or accepted. And some decide not to get married for kingdom reasons. But if you're capable of growing into the largeness of marriage, do it.' (Matthew 19:12, MSG)

It is important that we assure our children that if they choose, for one reason or another, not to marry, they can certainly live a cheerful, contented life. Although most marry, all do not. The goal for all of us is to align ourselves with God's will; this is where we will feel most fulfilled. We need to keep our eyes fixed upon Jesus. The goal is not necessarily a marriage relationship but a relationship with Christ Jesus.

A Wedding Is Time for Celebration

How well this is seen at the wedding in Cana described in John 2:1-10. Here, Jesus turned water into the best wine near the end of the celebration, when the cheapest wine was usually served. This wedding celebration is the setting for Jesus' first recorded miracle.

Sexual Warnings

- ➢ "[Abstain] from sexual immorality..." (Acts 15:20b).
- ➢ "Let us walk properly as in the daytime, not in orgies and drunkenness, not in sexual immorality and sensuality..." (Romans 13:13a).

- ➤ "Flee from sexual immorality" (1 Corinthians 6:18a).

- ➤ "We must not indulge in sexual immorality" (1Corinthians 10:8a).

- ➤ "But sexual immorality and all impurity or covetousness must not even be named among you, as is proper among saints" (Ephesians 5:3).

- ➤ "For this is the will of God, your sanctification: that you abstain from sexual immorality" (1 Thessalonians 4:3).

Keep Marriage Pure

"Marriage should be honored by all, and the marriage bed kept pure" (Hebrews 13:4a, NIV). Even after marriage the word pure is used to describe the way a married couple should act. This passage, as well as all of those above, make it quite clear that the Bible does indeed have a sexual ethic: God gave the good gift of sex to be used only within marriage as a marriage covenant renewal, to bond a couple more closely together, for marital pleasure, for comfort, to bring children into a family, and to celebrate love.

Believe God

God gave us His Word, the Bible, where He has made clear His design for every facet of life, including sex. But we must believe in His Son or His Word will fall on rocky soil. This is true for our children, too. Pray for believing hearts for your children. Only the believing heart has Christ's Spirit dwelling within. We cannot obey God on our own. Only Christ in us replaces an "ought to" attitude with a "want to" attitude. Our obedience stems from gratitude for all Christ has done for us.

Chapter 15

WHY IS SEX RESERVED FOR MARRIAGE?

And now the burning question: "Why did God say sex is only for marriage between a man and a woman?" Why would a good God give this powerful, wonderful, fun gift of sex and then say *wait* until marriage to use this gift? By using sex as God intended, one is protected from many sorrows and pains and becomes the beneficiary of His provision of joy and fulfillment. Further, in using sex as God intended, we participate in a unique way in the love Christ has for His church—we find an intimate space, a haven and a place of deep peace and acceptance.

People who have done it both ways know the difference. Tim Keller, senior pastor of the Redeemer Presbyterian Church in New York City, reflects upon couples who have been sexually active as singles but are now in committed marriages. They know these are two "radically different things."[126] A sexual relationship within the commitment of marriage brings security, contentment, joy and satisfaction; casual, non-committed sex produces scars.

165

Protection From Emotional Consequences

Gordon Hugenberger has stated that no matter what people think, when two people engage in sexual intercourse "it is not just nothing—no, something profound happens."[127] It is a profound union of two people, intended to be an enduring, unbreakable bond. Think of what happens when trying to separate two pieces of a whole that are bonded (glued) together. Terrible ripping results. A bond is a strong connection, not intended to be broken. When couples break up after experiencing this "something profound," it hurts and leaves lasting emotional scars. This is affirmed by a report in the *American Journal of Preventive Medicine:* "Early sexual activity and multiple partners are associated with pain and suffering from broken relationships, a sense of betrayal and abandonment, confusion about romantic feelings, altered self-esteem, depression, and impaired ability to form healthy long-term relationships."[128]

During sexual arousal and intercourse several hormones are released. Bonding of the couple is one of the intended effects of the hormonal release. Since we were designed by God for one sexual partner, when involved with multiple partners the effect of the bonding hormones becomes more and more diluted, making a lasting, intimate relationship harder and harder to achieve.[129] Think of the emotional scarring that results when couples, particularly teens, break off their relationship after they have initiated sex. Studies show that sixty-one percent of teens break up within three months after initiating sex in their relationship. Eighty percent of teens break up within six months after initiating sex.[130] This scarring is especially painful when sex has been engaged in for the purpose of finding

166

intimacy (one of the major reasons adolescents engage in sexual activity).[131]

To graphically illustrate this scarring, cut two hearts from heavy poster board. Have your son/daughter glue these together with Super Glue (or a good bonding glue). Hold them together for a few moments until well bonded. After about 15 minutes have your teen pull them apart. When ripped, the hearts should show significant damage on the glued sides with the outsides remaining undamaged. Point out to your teen that when you view these hearts from the outside there is no visible scarring. This is analogous to their friends who may be "sleeping around" and say that sex is no big deal, they are fine. But turn the heart pieces over (view the inside) and one can see significant scarring representing the betrayal, abandonment, impaired ability to form healthy long-term relationships, etc. mentioned above.[132]

There is no condom for the heart.

When we break God's commandments we are demonstrating a spirit of rebellion and this rebellion can follow us into marriage making marital intimacy difficult.

Compare the following two Scripture passages:

It is God's will that you should be sanctified: that you should avoid sexual immorality; that each of you should learn to control his own body in a way that is holy and honorable, not in passionate lust.... (1 Thessalonians 4:3-5a, NIV)

The husband should fulfill his marital duty to his wife, and likewise the wife to her husband. The wife's body does not belong to her alone but also to her husband. In the same way, the husband's body does not belong to him alone but also to his wife. Do not deprive each other.... (1 Corinthians 7:3-5a, NIV)

In her book *Liberated through Submission*, P.B. Wilson suggests: "The same spirit of rebellion that demands sex before marriage will refuse sex after marriage.... [Disobeying] God's commandment in Thessalonians appears to be preparing us to disobey the one in Corinthians."[133]

Using sex as God intended protects us from many painful, long-term emotional consequences.

Protection From Physical Consequences

Sexually transmitted diseases may change as medical science comes up with new treatments and vaccines, but as some are "cured" others will be discovered. When we act against the way we are made we will face physical consequences. "People who sin sexually sin against their own bodies" (1 Corinthians 6:18c, GW). Christ cares deeply for our bodies—He gave His life to redeem us, body and soul. "Who you are in your [earthly] body is meaningfully related to who you will be in your resurrection body."[134]

Sexual immorality harms the body on many different levels because of the oneness nature of sex: "...and the two will become one flesh" (Matthew 19:5). Sexual union is not just a satisfying of physical desire, it is a union of the physical, spiritual and emotional parts of two individuals and it is designed to result in an enduring bond. Trying to satisfy only self, sexually, can actually destroy self.

God did not make our bodies for fornication but designed marriage as a remedy. Unlike other sins, "...which are outside the body..." according to the 1 Corinthians 6 passage, fornication does damage to our bodies; it defiles the body which was designed to be a member of Christ and the temple of the Holy Spirit.

Protection From Spiritual Consequences

Continual disregard for God's moral laws has severe consequences because the spiritual and moral cannot be separated. "Do not be deceived: neither the sexually immoral, nor idolaters, nor adulterers...will inherit the kingdom of God" (From 1 Corinthians 6:9b-10). That is, if we continue to reject and disobey God's laws we will not be part of God's kingdom.

Note verse 11 which states that this is what some of us *were*. God majors in grace and forgiveness. The Spirit is at work in us causing repentance, then ushering in the fruit of repentance. By God's grace we become wounded healers—as we recognize and confess our sin, we are much more able to help our children, and others, deal with their temptations.

Protection From Sin's Deceit

Obeying God's design for sex protects us from the deceit of sin. Hebrews 11:25 tells us that sin is pleasurable...for a season. The Bible is refreshingly honest! How differently we would act if sin were immediately unpleasant. If it were, in order to avoid pain, we would sin a whole lot less. Instead, sin can be pleasurable at first, and maybe even for awhile, deceiving us by blinding us for a time to its consequences. But its pleasure wears out over time, revealing the true consequences of our disobedience: "Immorality puts us in opposition to God's purposes—physically, spiritually and psychologically— and the world of evil then overwhelms and controls."[135]

Jane tells how this worked in her life. As a young single woman in her late twenties she was traveling abroad alone. She met a man on a train who planned to stay in the same city as her for the night. They went to dinner together and ended the evening in a sexual encounter. It was very romantic, just what is often modeled in the movies.

In thinking about this several years later, after coming to an understanding of her immorality, she wondered how she'd frame this to her children. How could she lie and say it wasn't pleasurable? As she was thinking this thought, a quiet internal voice prompted her to remember not just the encounter, but its aftermath. Jane went on to recall her quick emotional deterioration—what had at first seemed romantic and pleasurable resulted in deep feelings of emptiness, dirtiness and hopelessness. Yes, evil overwhelmed and controlled her life for awhile.

The 21st century has seen a tremendous rise in loneliness, dissatisfaction and confusion in the sexual realm.

Jenny, the lead character in the movie *An Education*, consented to have sex on her 16th birthday with a man she hardly knew. She had no idea, for example, that he was a married man. She obviously found sex very disappointing compared to what she had expected. She comments: "All that poetry, all those songs about something that lasts no time at all."[136]

The beginning of sin can be compared to a small hole in a dam—for a season it seems like no big deal. But the pressure builds, pushing on that little hole until, eventually, the whole dam is brought down. Evil overwhelms and controls as the season runs its course and sin's once-hidden results become apparent. Sin is deceptive and its consequences painful. God calls us to save sex for marriage in order to avoid the overwhelming control of evil.

Protection From the Consequences of Sexual Sin

One can see the enormous consequences of sexual sin by looking at King David's adultery. Upon confession and repentance of his sin, King David was immediately forgiven by God for his adultery with Bathsheba (see 2 Samuel 11 and Psalm 51). Nevertheless, God did not spare him the consequences of his disobedience. Four of King David's sons died as a direct or indirect result. The first to die was the baby which was conceived in the adulterous act between David and Bathsheba. That child died shortly after birth.

The second to die was Amnon, who raped his half sister Tamar. King David did not punish this act and Amnon remained unrepentant. Eventually, Tamar's brother Absalom took matters into his own hands and killed Amnon. Absalom went on to incite a coup against David's rule, but in the process Absalom was killed, David's third son to die. Because Absalom was David's favorite son, his death was particularly painful for David. The following verse pulls us into David's heart-rending response to the news of his favorite son's death: "O my son Absalom, my son, my son Absalom!

Would I had died instead of you, O Absalom, my son, my son!" (2 Sam 18:33b).

The fourth son to die was Adonijah who also attempted a failed coup, this time against King Solomon's reign. David paid a heavy price and suffered long-term consequences for his disobedience.

Cheryl, a woman in her early 60s, visited an Ear, Nose and Throat Clinic presenting a hearing loss which had been getting worse over the last few years. She wondered if anything could be done. This was at a teaching hospital and she was seen by a couple of residents. They examined her, did a hearing test, and drew some blood because her hearing loss looked suspicious. The blood results came back positive for syphilis. Cheryl was a dignified woman, married to one man for over 40 years. She attended church regularly and lived a conservative life style. When the blood test came back, the residents struggled with how to tell this dignified older woman that her hearing loss was due to syphilis. Neither resident wanted to be the one to tell her, so they finally flipped a coin. The loser, with great embarrassment and trepidation, shared this difficult news with Cheryl. When he told her, she responded:

"Oh, yes, I know that. I was infected at birth by my mother. Is that the reason for my hearing loss?"

"Yes," he replied. "Unfortunately, your hearing loss will continue to get worse until you become totally deaf."

The painful consequences that often result from sexual sin usually affect more than just the perpetrator. Sometimes, innocent people face years of suffering.

Reserving Sex for Marriage Provides for Us

Using sex God's way provides joy, beauty and blessing. A marriage counselor once stated that in all of his counseling experience (hundreds of couples), no one had ever said they regretted the level of purity they were able to maintain before marriage; but countless couples regretted their premarital sexual activity.[137]

A study in the December 28, 2010 *Journal of Family Psychology* reported that couples who waited until marriage to have sex were the most satisfied with the quality of sex, whereas couples who had sex soon after meeting had the worst relationship outcomes. "Regardless of religiosity, waiting helps the relationship form better communication processes, and these help improve long-term stability and relationship satisfaction."[138]

The following two testimonies paint a beautiful picture of marriage entered into with sexual purity.

> I waited 10 years for my wife. I waited seven years as a friend, two as a boyfriend, and one as a fiancé—patiently, constantly, even downright stubbornly. I waited in the hormonal agony of electrified minutes as I sat next to her on a couch and I waited for months in the slow deep ache of a thousand miles away from her. I waited as I did not kiss her, caress her, or have sex with her. I waited in all the "don'ts" and "won'ts"—in the goodnights and goodbyes, sincerely's, loves, and see ya's. That's about 3,650 days of waiting!—of knowing that I liked this girl, then knowing that I loved this girl, then knowing that I wanted to marry this girl—day upon day upon day. Why? Why would

anyone wait that long? Well, instead of trying to tell you, let me try to show you.

See, I'm typing this testimony at 10:20 at night here in our apartment bedroom. The room is softly lit by the bedside lamp that my wife is using to read as she sits snuggly tucked in bed. I can hear her rustling and shifting under our blue blanket and purple comforter, occasionally turning pages in her book. And I know her so well—I can perfectly picture what she is doing with her elbow and wrist as I hear her yawn; I know just how her nose crinkles and how her jaw opens slightly to one side. I love her! She is my wife! It's just the two of us here, in a space that's perfectly and peacefully ours. We don't need to justify or explain ourselves to anyone or to our own consciences; we are married; we are one because we have been made one through the covenant of marriage. Our marriage, our union, and in it our sexuality and intimacy, are beautiful to a large extent because of this peace and guiltlessness. There is nothing dark about it; we have no secrets to keep; everything is done in the light of the Lord's blessing, and He certainly is a gracious and good God.

Behind me, she's beginning to shift just a little more frequently, ready for me to come to bed. To our bed. I would have waited twenty years for this!

In my mind, our wedding day is seriously the most blessed day of my life. And after all of the hubbub died down and we'd ridden off into the sunset to a little bed and breakfast, I was covered with the most profound sense of peace in knowing that—though we had struggled, yes, and though we had failed and hurt one another at times—the Lord had given us strength to persevere and preserve ourselves for each other. I always thought I would be nervous on my wedding night, but walking out of the bathroom that evening my eyes met those of the man whom I'd loved for six years, and whom I knew was committed to me for life. I didn't have to worry about how I looked or if we were any good at any of this.... We knew that we belonged to one another and our committed love gave us a deep trust in one another.

Marital Sex: a Symbol Pointing to Christ's Love

God intends marriage to reflect Christ's love for His church. Through the intimacy of sex in marriage, God is showing us Christ's love in terms we can understand. "Sexual desire," states Wesley Hill in his book *Washed and Waiting,* "is a taste or analogy of what it must mean for God himself to yearn for a relationship with us."[139] This doesn't mean that Christ's love for His people is sexual. Rather, sex in marriage is a very powerful symbol pointing to Christ's love; the two things are different and yet have similarities.

A symbol seldom resembles what it is pointing to. Consider a wedding ring. My wedding ring doesn't look at all like my husband: he is not round, nor does he have a hole in his middle. However, my ring is a circle with no end symbolizing my commitment to love my husband until death parts us. My ring points to my love for my husband and tells the world that I am married and committed to him.

This symbolism is somewhat mysterious—we cannot fully explain it. But we know it when we see it. That is, we know that the deep, devoted, long-time love of a married couple reflects more than just the two of them. It points to Christ and His love, a love which is totally captivating.

The Apostle Paul articulates this in Ephesians Chapter 5: "'Therefore a man shall leave his father and mother and hold fast to his wife, and the two shall become one flesh.' This mystery is profound, and I am saying that it refers to Christ and the church" (Ephesians 5:31-32). In this passage, Paul starts talking about human marriage but moves quickly to "this mystery" of Christ and His love for the church. In some unexplainable way a committed marriage shows the world the way Christ loves His own. Jesus' love for His own is not sexual, but He "knows" us and commits to love us in a deeply profound and eternal way.

Consider some parallels between Christ's love and married love:

Christ died for us while we were still sinners. He didn't wait for us to get perfect and He promises to forgive us when we repent. When a couple stand together ready to be married, they are not even capable of loving each other perfectly, but they commit to each other: "We promise to love each other for better or worse, in sickness and in health...." There are times when we are not very lovable, times when life is tough; but restoration in our relationship is possible because of our committed love for one another.

Christ began a "forever" relationship with us and He will not let us go. The marriage vows include the promise to love each other "for as long as we both shall live." Christ will not give up on us. He will not "dump" us for a better bet. He will never forsake us. There is a oneness described in Christ's love and married love. Christ's prayer for His church is that "they [His people] may all be one, just as you, Father, are in me, and I in you, that they also may be in us..." (John 17:21). One way that marriage is described is God making the two one.

Marriage and sex go together in God's mind. If marriage is a covenant (and many believe it is), sex is the sealing of that covenant and a covenant renewal every time a married couple has sex.

Tim Keller, pastor of Redeemer Presbyterian Church in New York City, stated that sex in marriage and communion (the Lord's Supper) have the same role. Sex is a renewing of the marriage covenant between husband and wife as the Lord's Supper is a renewing of the covenant between God and the believer.[140] Similar admonitions are given by the Apostle Paul if either (sex or communion) is undertaken in an unworthy manner:

> Flee from sexual immorality. Every other sin a person commits is outside the body, but the sexually immoral person sins against his own body. (1 Corinthians 6:18)

> Whoever, therefore, eats the bread or drinks the cup of the Lord in an unworthy manner will be guilty concerning the body and blood of the Lord. (1 Corinthians 11: 27)

In the first passage we sin against our own body, and in the second passage we call down curses upon ourselves.[141]

Marriage and sex go together in God's mind.

Sex in marriage is a symbol pointing to the reality of Christ's eternal love for His own. When the reality is established, when we are with the Lord after death, then the symbol will no longer be needed. Jesus says that there is no marriage in Heaven (Matthew 22:30). Then, all those who trust Jesus will "know" every other one, even as we are "known"—a deeply intimate, non-sexual knowing, caring and loving for all of eternity.

Let's look at some aspects of Jesus' love for His own as viewed in the following three composite pictures taken from Jesus' time on earth.

The Bridegroom: We had planned carefully for our wedding, but more people came than we expected. What a celebration it was! Jesus, His mother, and some of His disciples also came. I heard from one of our stewards, after our wedding day, that we had run out of wine and my parents were feeling very embarrassed, even humiliated, knowing they had not prepared well enough. They thought the only thing people would remember about our wedding was that the wine ran out. That, however, is not what happened. The steward told me that as he was trying to decide what to do, Jesus came to him and told him to fill six jars with water, then to take some to the master of the feast. I remember that the master of the feast came to me and commented on the exquisite quality of the wine that was being served near the end of our celebration. Now I understand, from what our steward told me, that Jesus turned water into wine. He cared so much for us that He provided the best and prevented our utter humiliation. Oh, how He loves us.[142]

Woman One: Indeed, how He loves us! I had given up on living a moral life. My husband and I were just not getting along. He treated me with such indifference; he didn't seem to care if I was home or not. How different it was with my neighbor. He treated me as if I were a queen: he listened to me, he encouraged me, he made me feel beautiful. We got closer and closer until, one day, it just happened. I knew what we were doing was wrong, but I just couldn't help myself. Then the nightmare began. Bursting into my neighbor's bedroom came some of the leaders of the synagogue. They must have been watching us and waiting to catch us. As they dragged me out of bed, I was only able to grab a sheet to cover myself. They half dragged me to the Temple and placed me in the middle of a circle of men and told Jesus of catching me in the very act of adultery. I knew that my life was about to end very painfully. The punishment for adultery was stoning. I was numb with dread and terror, not able to follow what was going on around me when, out of the haze of pain and humiliation, I realized that Jesus was speaking to me. He was asking me where my accusers had gone. Had no one condemned me? I looked around and saw only Jesus. "No, Lord, no one has condemned me." He looked at me with such amazing kindness and love, then said,

"Neither do I condemn you; go, and from now on sin no more."

I was a changed woman from then on. Jesus had cared deeply for me, He had rescued me, He forgave me, He set my feet onto a totally new, obedient path. He loved me.[143]

Woman Two: I traveled with Jesus through much of His teaching ministry. I heard Him talk about how much He loved us. He said He loved us with an everlasting love. He assured us that we were His, that no one was able to snatch us from His hand. When loved as He loved us I was always looking for ways I could serve Him. I knew the religious leaders didn't like Jesus. They didn't like what He was teaching, but I didn't expect them to kill Him! The synagogue leaders had Him arrested, falsely charged and crucified. I don't understand anything anymore. He said He loved me with an everlasting love. But how can He love me if He's dead?

Now, only one thing is left that I can do for Him and that is to anoint His body and properly prepare it for burial. We were unable to do that just after He died, so after the Sabbath we planned to be at His tomb very early, just as soon as it grew light. How utterly devastated I was when we arrived at the tomb only to find it empty. Someone must have moved His body! But why? I desperately wanted to do one last thing for Him, for His body; but now I couldn't because it wasn't in the tomb. Stooping down to look into the tomb, I saw two men in white sitting where His body should have been. They asked me why I was weeping and I told them.

"They have taken away my Lord, and I do not know where they have laid Him."

Then I looked around and saw the gardener standing near. He, too, asked me why I was weeping, who was I seeking.

"Sir," I said, "if you have carried Him away, tell me where you have laid Him, and I will take Him away."

And then it happened: the One I supposed to be the gardener called me by name: "Mary." Much was communicated in that one word—my name, Mary: an everlasting love that no one can ever take away. I am His and He is mine. Oh, love...such amazing love![144]

Now, compare Christ's love to the love shown by the following three couples.

Couple One: They had been married for more than 60 years but Sylvia's physical care had exceeded the state standards allowing her to remain with

John in assisted living. The head nurse informed John, with a great deal of sorrow, that Sylvia had to be moved to a nursing home. John accompanied her to her new place of care but did not leave her alone any longer than absolutely necessary. Each day, immediately after breakfast, John left his place and drove the few miles to where Sylvia was. He spent all day with her, by her bedside or sitting with her in the dining room, sometimes spending the entire afternoon just trying to get a cup of soup spooned into Sylvia's mouth. He cared for her and loved her as he had promised, until death parted them.

The following couple modeled marriage so well that family, friends, and community members knew they were committed "until death do us part."

Couple Two: When Gordon and Norma Yeager were in an automobile accident, after seventy-two years of marriage, they were taken to the nearby hospital where even the nurses in the Intensive Care Unit knew this couple was not to be separated. They were admitted to the same room where they held hands for the remaining hours of their lives.

"They just loved being together," said their daughter. "We were very blessed, honestly, that they went this way." She noted that neither one of them would have wanted to survive the other.

Their son tells of the last hour of his mother's life: "It was really strange: they were holding hands and dad stopped breathing, but I couldn't figure out what was going on because the heart monitor [his father's] was still going...." One of the nurses explained that, although Gordon had died, because he and his wife were holding hands the heart impulses from Norma were showing up on Gordon's monitor—Gordon's monitor was "still getting her heartbeat through him."[145]

What a powerful example of the two becoming one.

Couple Three: Robertson McQuilkin's love for his wife is yet another example of the "for better, for worse, in sickness and in health" kind of love that both models biblical marriage and points to Jesus' love for his own. When Muriel developed Alzheimer's at a relatively young age, the only place she felt safe was in his presence. Robertson was then the president of Columbia Bible College and Seminary and a well-known New Testament theologian. When Muriel's illness progressed to a place where she could not be left alone, Robertson resigned his position. Many of their friends tried to persuade him to find a good nursing home, a place where all of his wife's physical needs would be well met. But Robertson knew this would terrify her. "I made a promise on our wedding day and I intend to keep it," he said. The following passage from Robertson's book *A Promise Kept* reveals the challenges, and the impact, of his commitment.

> Our flight was delayed in Atlanta and we had to wait a couple of hours. Now that's a challenge. Every few minutes, the same questions, the same answers about what we're doing here, when are we going home? And every few minutes we'd take a fast-paced walk down the terminal in earnest search of—what? Muriel had always been a speed walker. I had to jog to keep up with her! An attractive woman executive type sat across from us, working diligently on her computer. Once, when we returned from an excursion, she said something, without looking up from

her papers. Since no one else was nearby I assumed she had spoken to me or at least mumbled in protest of our constant activity.

"Pardon?" I asked.

"Oh," she said, "I was just asking myself, 'Will I ever find a man to love me like that?'"[146]

That woman saw a man who loved his wife the way Christ loves the church and she wanted that kind of love.

> *From heaven He came and sought her*
> *To be His holy Bride;*
> *With His own blood He bought her,*
> *And for her life He died.*[147]

Being Real and Honest

Chapter 16

MYTHS OF BEING GROWN UP

Do you remember, as a teen, thinking how you just couldn't wait to grow up so you could do what you wanted? Did you ever say or think: "Why do you need to know where I'm going or when I'll be home?" Did you ever take comfort in thoughts like "One day I'll be in charge," or "When I grow up I'll never have to say I'm sorry"? Often, we think that when we grow up we will be able to throw off the shackles of rules and laws and be truly independent, no longer living in a family fishbowl where everyone sees what we are doing. We think we will be able to do what we want, when we want and with whom we want, and no one else need know.

Isn't this an echo of what Adam and Eve felt in the garden when they decided to throw off God's law and decide for themselves what was right and wrong? Did they think they could be independent of God? They did not attain independence, freedom from all restraint, and neither do we, even as adults. Unless we are hermits we live in community, and the closer the relationship the more interdependent we are. For this reason the things we expect of our children we should also expect of ourselves.

TALK

Susan asked her teenage son John where he was going and when he'd be back.

"Why do you always need to know where I'm going?" John replied irritably.

"I seem to recall that every week you bring your calendar to my desk and ask to see my date book so you can write down where I'll be and when," Susan replied with as much calmness as a mom can when faced with a determined teen. "You want to know where I'm going to be. Can you understand that I'd like to know where you're going to be, too? A family works that way."

That was the last time John refused to share the where's and when's of his life. He got it.

What about times when we lose our cool because of fatigue or stress? If we try to deny our anger or misplace blame, our children know we are wrong.

Mary, a harried mother of six, dropped her kids off at school with a promise to pick them up after the day's activities. She was almost always late. When her children tried to say anything about always having to wait, she'd get angry and give them a litany of what she had to do in a day and add that they should be grateful to have someone willing to pick them up. A simple apology would have gone a long way.

Being grown up means we readily apologize to our children and confess when we're wrong.

Children know when parents are in the wrong. If no amends are sought, it leaves hostility and discontent in the hearts of children. But if a

188

parent admits, "I was wrong when I did _____. Please forgive me," it is amazing how that small sentence defuses a hostile environment and results in a feeling that all is again right with the world. Apologizing to our children is something parents can practice as soon as their children understand language. By doing so you are not only doing what is right, you are modeling a humble spirit and creating an open atmosphere where all can confess their mistakes, wrongs and sins.

What are we modeling to our children—Christ's righteousness or our own? If we never admit to error we model self-righteousness, which is a lie. "None is righteous, no, not one" (Romans 3:10). As we daily admit our errors and ask for others' forgiveness, we have opportunity to explain how we, as imperfect people, can have right standing before a holy God. It is Christ's righteousness that we want to model, and that can only be done with a humble heart which readily admits to error and sin.

Being grown up means we humbly model Christ's righteousness, not our own.

Reading between the lines of Scripture, it appears that King David felt that since he had "blown it" sexually he could not hold his children accountable when they committed sexual sin. Following his adultery with Bathsheba, David's son Amnon raped his half sister Tamar (2 Samuel 13). When King David heard about this, he did nothing to deal with Amnon, imposing no discipline of any kind when the law required Amnon's death. As king, David could have extended mercy instead of death; but he did nothing, never even talking about this with Amnon. One can almost hear David thinking: I did the same thing and worse; I committed adultery then arranged the murder of my good friend, Bathsheba's husband. How can I possibly discipline my son when I was shown mercy?

David's heart, however, was very different from Amnon's heart. When the prophet Nathan confronted David in 2 Samuel 12, David saw his sin and immediately repented. Amnon, on the other hand, went away with a hardened heart. Sometimes we need to be the prophet Nathan to our children, helping them to see their sin. We also need to pray that they will quickly repent. The fact that we may have committed similar sins in our past is no excuse for being passive in the face of our children's sin.

Being grown up means holding our children responsible for their sin.

If I humble myself will I lose my parental authority? Jesus, Lord of heaven and earth, did not lose His authority when he humbled himself.

> Jesus, knowing that the Father had given all things into his hands, and that he had come from God and was going back to God, rose from supper. He laid aside his outer garments, and taking a towel, tied it around his waist. Then he poured water into a basin and began to wash the disciples' feet and to wipe them with the towel that was wrapped around him. (John 13:3-5)

Was His authority any less after He washed the feet of the disciples than it had been before He washed their feet?

It was after he had grown up and married that Robert, sitting at his parents' dinner table, asked this question: "If you could go back and change one thing in your parenting, what would it be?"

His parents thought for a bit and replied, "We'd change many things if we had it to do again." Then they asked him: "What would you change in our parenting, if you could?"

He responded, "Yes, you did a lot of things wrong, but one thing you did right—you were always humble and always willing to ask forgiveness."

Edwin Brown tells the following story:

As I grew up, my father and I had many serious arguments. One day, when I was 17, we had a particularly violent one. I said to him, "This is the straw that breaks the camel's back. I'm leaving and I will never return." So saying, I went to the house and packed a bag. My mother begged me to stay, but I was too mad and upset to listen. I left her crying at the doorway.

As I left the yard and was about to pass through the gate, I heard my father call to me.

"Frank," he said, "I know that a large share of the blame for your leaving rests with me. For this I am deeply sorry. But I want you to know that if you should ever wish to return to our home, you'll always be welcome. And I'll try to be a better father to you. I want you to know that I'll always love you."

I said nothing, but went to the bus station and bought a ticket to a hundred miles from nowhere. But as I sat in the bus watching the miles go by I began to think about the words of my father. I began to realize how much maturity, how much goodness, how much love it had required for him to do what he had done. He had apologized. He had invited me back and he left the words ringing in my ears: "I love you."

It was then I realized the next move was up to me. I knew the only way I could ever find peace with myself was to demonstrate to him the same kind of maturity, goodness and love that he had demonstrated toward me.

I got off the bus. I bought a return ticket home and went back. I arrived just before midnight. I entered the house and turned on the light. There in our rocking chair sat my father, his head in his hands. As he looked up and saw me, he rose from the chair and we rushed into each other's arms.

That was the beginning of a new relationship between my father and me. Those last years that I was home were among the happiest of my life....[148]

That father learned to model humility and, in the process, won back his son.

> ***Being grown up means that we as parents learn,***
> ***by God's grace, to model servant leadership for***
> ***our children, just as Jesus did for His disciples.***

Chapter 17

TELLING THE TRUTH

Children/teens are interested in our lives and how we lived when we were their age. But before we can answer their questions honestly we need to be honest with ourselves. We need to admit to ourselves what we did and where we sinned. It wasn't a friend, it was a boy/girlfriend. It wasn't a mistake, it was a choice. It wasn't just cleaning out tissue, it was a decision to deny life. Next, we need to go to our merciful God and repent of our sin, knowing that Jesus died to cleanse us from our sin, to make it as if we never sinned.

Before we can guide our children in an area where we have sinned, we also need to be healed ourselves. We need to ask Christ to heal us and make us whole: "...though your sins are like scarlet, they shall be as white as snow" (Isaiah 1:18b). In this way we become wounded healers.

We can come to Christ because "we do not have a high priest who is unable to sympathize with our weaknesses, but one who in every respect has been tempted as we are, yet without sin. Let us then with confidence draw near to the throne of grace, that we may receive mercy and find grace to help in time of need" (Hebrews 4:15-16).

Our Sin Used for the Good

One of the ways in which God will work for the good in all things (even our sexual sin) is to enable us to lead our children in the way they should go, to have influence in their lives and encourage them to follow God's way—not the way we went, not a generational bent, but a better way:

> The LORD, the LORD, a God merciful and gracious, slow to anger, and abounding in steadfast love and faithfulness, keeping steadfast love for thousands, forgiving iniquity and transgression and sin, but who will by no means clear the guilty, visiting the sins of the fathers on the children and the children's children, to the third and the fourth generation. (Exodus 34:6-7)

That is good news! Even generational bents can be forgiven when recognition and repentance take place. But if not confessed and repented of, all too often children and children's children may fall into the same sin.

Is It Guilt or Regret?

False guilt—feeling guilty for that which God has already forgiven—can stymie relationships. "I wish I could take that back." Ask yourself this question: Is it guilt or is it regret?

Guilt is the awareness of having done wrong with an associated heavy burden of self condemnation. Regret is feeling sorry and sad about something previously done, but without an albatross hanging around our neck. Guilt should drive us to the cross with a heart of repentance. At the cross, confess your sin and ask for forgiveness, then leave your sin behind. Jesus died for you to make you as if you had never sinned. Jesus did the hard work so that we can be forgiven and cleansed.

"If we confess our sins, he is faithful and just to forgive us our sins and to cleanse us from all unrighteousness" (1 John 1:9). If we can't let go of our sin, it's as if we are saying Jesus hasn't done enough! And if we won't release it after asking for forgiveness, it can interfere with all of our close relationships, even to the point of paralyzing us. This is especially true in the case of sexual sin.

Be reminded of this: "As far as the east is from the west, so far does he remove our transgressions from us" (Psalm 103:12). Does east ever meet west? That's how far God has removed our sin from us! Corrie ten Boom adds: "When I confessed them [my sins] to the Father, Jesus Christ washed them in His blood. They are now cast into the deepest sea and a sign is put up that says, NO FISHING ALLOWED."[149] Once you've repented and asked for forgiveness, accept that the penalty has been paid by Jesus. Then, if you slide back into guilt, think about images such as "being white as snow," a wedding dress, a bride "without spot or blemish" prepared for her groom (Jesus), or the deepest part of the ocean where God buried your sin. Ask the Holy Spirit to change your thinking, to help you to jettison guilt. Regret, we will live with—it goes with not being perfect; but guilt can be given to Jesus. When truly given to Him you will recognize the breathtaking promise of Romans 8:28: "And we know that for those who love God *all* things work together for good, for those who are called according to his purpose" (emphasis added). God can even use our sin for good.

An example of retained guilt (rather than regret) following forgiveness can be seen in the story of Joseph's brothers in Genesis 50. You'll recall that Joseph was sold into slavery by his brothers, later imprisoned, and finally elevated to the position of prime minister of Egypt, second in power only to Pharaoh. Seventeen years after selling Joseph and assuming him dead, his brothers come face to face with him in a dramatic confrontation. When Joseph revealed himself they were shocked and, rightly, afraid. But Joseph said "...do not be distressed or angry with yourselves because you sold me here, for God sent me before you to preserve life" (Genesis 45:5).

Joseph assumed his brothers would accept his forgiveness and put their murderous behavior behind them. However, many years later, after the death of their father Jacob, Joseph's brothers still felt guilty and afraid of Joseph's possible retaliation. They sent this message to Joseph: "Your father gave this command before he died, 'Say to Joseph, Please forgive the transgression of your brothers and their sin, because they did evil to you'" (Genesis 50:16-17). When Joseph became aware of this he wept and once again assured them of his total forgiveness: "Do not fear, for am I in the place of God? As for you, you meant evil against me, but God meant it for good, to bring it about that many people should be kept alive, as they are today...thus he comforted them and spoke kindly to them" (Genesis 50:19-21).

Sharing our regrets with our children can be a powerful teaching tool, but guilt should be left with our sins at the foot of the cross. Matthew Henry says our sins "shall never be laid to our charge, nor rise up in judgment against us. If we thoroughly forsake them, God will thoroughly forgive them."[150] And God does more than forgive us: "For those who are in Christ, God is no longer the Judge who condemns us but the Father who adopts us into His family."[151]

Telling Our Kids the Truth

When the subject of sex has been an open topic in families—both in early body part and function discussions and, later, in talking about healthy sexuality—children are apt to ask: "What about you, Mom/Dad? Were you virgins when you got married?" If you haven't expected this question or given any thought to its response, this could result in a crisis moment. Be aware that once the question is asked, no matter what you answer or don't answer, the truth will be obvious. Be honest answering this question and you will greatly enhance trust and respect from your children. This as an opportunity, so don't blow it!

If the answer is "Yes, we were virgins when we married," if you haven't already done so, tell your children how you met, about your courtship, how you knew you loved each other, the story of your engagement. Each of you tell your story because your perspectives are different and it is fun to hear both sides. Be prepared to share the joy of your wedding day—the anticipation, the beauty of purity, the covenant you made, and your anticipation of sealing the covenant of marriage. Be prepared to share with your children the difficulties of making it to marriage as a virgin, the temptations you faced and how you handled them.

If the answer is "No," no matter what you say, or don't say your kids will know the answer. Who would have trouble telling their children that they were virgins when they married? The problem comes when the answer is negative. If you try to evade the question or get angry (telling them, in essence, it's none of their business), you are being disingenuous. You've presumably been encouraging your children to be open with you. Won't they think or say, "You want me to be honest with you but you won't be honest with me"? Furthermore, they will know the answer to their question is "No."

"Do you, my parents, hereby swear that you have never engaged in improper sexual relationships or activities before marriage?"

Pat and Jim, juniors in high school, are spending a lot of time together. Many times when Pat is expected home she shows up late. April, her mom, knows she has been with Jim and decides to have a talk with Pat.

It's after dinner and April is doing the dishes. Pat says she's going out for a while.

April: "Not now, you're not. We need to talk. You've been spending a lot of time with Jim lately. Just what are you doing when you're together?"

Pat, defensively: "What are we doing? Do you mean, are we doing 'it'? Mom, don't worry about what I'm doing. I'm sure it was just what you were doing at my age. I've seen the pictures of you and your high school boyfriend—in every one of them the two of you are crushed together and couldn't have gotten any closer if you had wanted. I'm sure you were doing stuff with him! I'm glad you brought this up, because I've wanted to ask you if you were a virgin when you and Dad got married."

April nearly chokes, gets red in the face, becomes defensive, and tries to claim that he wasn't a boyfriend, just a friend. Then she adds:

"I don't need to answer that. Have you forgotten you're the daughter and I'm the mother?"

"What is that supposed to mean?" Pat replies "Mom, get with it! You can't control everything in my life. And if you refuse to answer my question, why should I answer your question?"

What was the answer to the daughter's question? The answer was obviously no—April, the mom, was not a virgin. But April would not admit this. That would probably be the end of any further conversation about Pat's sexual behavior.

In a desperate attempt to prevent her daughter from getting too involved sexually, April will try to control Pat with a myriad of rules. "Don't do this" and "don't do that," attempts at external controls but without a relationship. This is seldom successful.

If this question is not answered, valuable teaching opportunities are lost. Teaching, even from the negative, can be powerful. You know the pain and consequences of your own behavior; try to help your child avoid these pitfalls. We need to remember that "all have sinned and fall short of the glory of God" (Romans 3:23). Besides, our children know we are not perfect, so don't try to hide sin.

Consider the same situation slightly modified. Pat is spending a good deal of time alone with Jim, and April is concerned. This time April tries to approach the conversation in a much softer way.

After school one day, April prepares Pat's favorite cookies and invites her to the table as she comes home. After enjoying small talk, cookies and milk, April brings up the subject of Pat and Jim's relationship. They proceed to have a civilized discussion about sex and boyfriends.

At one point Pat asks April if she ever talked with her mom about sex and boyfriends.

"No," April replies.

"Why not?" asks Pat.

"She stayed far away from the subject of sex. She seemed scared and ashamed."

Eventually Pat asks April the same question: "What about you and Dad? Were you virgins when you got married?"

This time April is calm and gentle as she answers. "I don't think it would help you to know that. After all, that was a private decision I had to make, and you are going to have to make that decision too."

Although less defensive, this response is still not helpful. The answer to the daughter's question is again, obviously, "No." Furthermore, when April tells Pat that the decision about sexual activity is Pat's to make and not any business of hers, April refuses to guide her daughter. Tragically, this shuts out any possibility of help, sound advice, and encouraging the thinking through of consequences.

Conversations between teens and a trusted other (a parent who loves them) can be very fruitful. Parents can guide their kids in discussion of how to remain pure and in setting up reasonable and helpful boundaries.

By not answering honestly parents miss opportunities to open dialog and build relationship with their child. And by not answering honestly parents miss opportunities to talk about the power of forgiveness and restoration because of Jesus Christ. Parents need to be prepared for this question; they need to discuss it together, agreeing on how they will answer. If they can't agree, one open and honest answer is better than none.

A young high school girl and her boyfriend grew closer and closer. Sex soon entered their relationship and she got pregnant. Oh, the panic that ensued when she missed her first period! She knew little about pregnancy and was only vaguely aware of the other early signs of pregnancy. She waited for another month and still no period. In desperation she finally turned to her mother, telling her that she thought she was pregnant. At that time, before abortion was legal, out-of-wedlock pregnancy was viewed as shameful. Far too ashamed to remain in the community, she did what many young girls of that era did: she went away to an "unwed mothers' home."

She just disappeared for several months, during which many and varied excuses were made for her absence. The baby was adopted upon delivery and the problem disappeared, or so they hoped.

The young woman returned home, finished high school, and married the man whose baby she had carried. They subsequently had other children. The existence of their firstborn was known to no one except the young woman, her mother, and her husband. It was a *big secret*. The subjects of sex and dating were never broached in the family for fear the secret might be exposed. The secret begot lies, lies begot other lies, and the marriage eventually broke up.

The children born after the marriage never knew about their other sibling until they were adults and their parents divorced. By then, the secret finally got too heavy for the father, and he told his adult children about the existence of their older sibling.

If the answer to the question is "No, I/we weren't virgin(s) when we married," a simple admission of "no" is what's required. Nothing is served by going into detail and sharing graphic images. But it would be helpful to identify the unforeseen consequences of not having acted as God calls us to. If you regret the choices you made, that would be helpful for your children to know. Tell them about the forgiveness you have received in Jesus Christ. Explain that your own history and its pain (if that is the case) compels you to guide, encourage and cheer them on.

Falling off the Throne

It is difficult to tell our children about our weaknesses and sin. We want others to think that we are good; even more, we want our children to think well of us. Some issues, however, like drug use and sex, need to be spoken of. We really are hampered in guiding our children if we are unwilling to be honest with them about these things.

Kids want to think their parents can do no wrong—at least this is true until adolescence when kids often reverse their thinking and believe nothing their parents do is right. As kids grow up they increasingly realize their parents are not perfect. Parents who insist on acting as if they are never wrong are apt to face skeptical, and even hostile, children.

Answering the "Were you virgins when you married?" question from your children will often usher in some painful moments. Be prepared to face the question head-on; think through your answer, be prepared to confess if appropriate, and then commit to walk with them through their disillusionment.

A young woman who had resisted the pressure of sex for many years finally met the man of her dreams. By the time she met him, the voices of the culture were overwhelming and she no longer understood why she shouldn't sleep with him if they planned to marry anyway. What, after all, was a piece of paper (marriage license)? Abortion was "legal" and she agreed to sleep with him with the understanding that if something happened they would abort. They used contraception but it didn't work and, much to her horror, she found herself pregnant. She was known as a "good girl." The two were planning on getting married but she did not want people silently counting from their marriage date and comparing it to the birth date of the oldest child. So she aborted her child.

They did marry and before long their next child was born. The Lord transformed the hearts of that couple, convicting them of their sin and showing them His mercy, because of the work of Jesus Christ on the cross.

After much prayer and Scripture study this couple decided not to keep this a secret but to be open, honest and humble with their children. Before any of the "heavy duty" sex and dating discussions ensued they wanted their children to know about their abortion. They elected to tell them as soon as they could understand so that in subsequent conversations the children would know that they were teaching God's way and not the way they had gone. The children of that family went into their marriages as virgins.

> *"He who conceals his transgressions will not prosper, but he who confesses and forsakes them will find compassion." (Proverbs 28:13, NASB)*

But being dethroned can be very painful and humbling.

Another couple, Mary and Joe, knew that there were dangers in waiting too long to tell their children about their abortion. It seemed to them that it would be best to inform their children as soon as they were able to understand, giving plenty of time for their children to digest the fact and hopefully be more responsive to their parents' guidance in later years. They agreed to look for the right time to tell them. For one of their children the time came when Mary was driving elementary school car pool. In the back of the car her daughter and several friends were talking about miscarriages, each one telling about the miscarriages their moms had had. Her daughter called to Mary from the back of the car,

"Mom, you had just one miscarriage, right?"

"I did have a miscarriage. We can talk about it when we get home."

When they got home, Mary and her daughter were alone and the time was right. Mary brought the subject up again and told her daughter that before they were married they became pregnant. There is just no way to soft peddle such a confession, so she simply said that she had aborted their child. The daughter, being well-schooled in the issues surrounding abortion, was shocked.

"You mean, you murdered your own child?"

"Yes," Mary admitted. "That's what happened."

Then she went on to engage her daughter in a poignant discussion of repentance and God's amazing grace and forgiveness. The daughter developed a deep respect for her parents and because of their humble honesty found it much easier in her later adolescence to talk about wrong things she had done. Many years later she commented:

"If you hadn't been honest with me, I wouldn't have been honest with you. But because you were open with me, I knew it was safe to share anything I needed to with you."

Only God is good, and our children need to understand this as soon as they are able. We need to disabuse them of the idea that their parents are perfect, sometimes by revealing our secrets.

Chapter 18

SECRETS

Secrets have many consequences and can have tremendous power. As long as we hold something secret, we do everything possible to guard against anyone finding out. So secrets beget other secrets, and lies are told to avoid or guard the truth we are hiding. But secrets can cause emotional and physical distress and cause us to do terrible things to cover up that which we do not want others to know.

Secrets Result in Emotional and Physical Distress

Secrets can cause emotional distress which may express itself in irritability, trouble sleeping, anger, and any number of other manifestations. Secrets can also cause physical pain. "For when I kept silent, my bones wasted away through my groaning all day long. For day and night your hand was heavy upon me; my strength was dried up as by the heat of summer" (Psalm 32:3-4).

Horrific acts may result when people try to cover up their sins. In 2 Samuel 11 we read about King David's adultery with Bathsheba, David's choosing to have intercourse with Uriah the Hittite's wife. When Bathsheba told David she was pregnant, King David called Bathsheba's husband in from the battlefield under the pretense of getting a firsthand report of the battle. His real motive was to get Uriah to sleep with his wife so that her pregnancy would be attributed to her husband and not the king. When this didn't work, because Uriah refused such comfort while the rest of the army was out fighting the battle, David arranged to have Uriah sent to the front lines, exposing him to certain death. After Uriah's death, David took Bathsheba to be his wife with the continued hope that no one would know that the baby was David's and had been conceived before they married.

How many abortions happen in order to cover up the fact of a pregnancy? One woman, single when she became pregnant, admitted years later that she did not want anyone to know she was having sex before she and her boyfriend were married, so she aborted her baby. In the earlier story of the two young medical students (found on page 117), their desire that "no one need ever know" about their abortion led to the mother's death.

Freedom in Unburdening Secrets

Coming clean is such a relief—no more looking over our shoulder and no more having to be careful about what we say. Once our sin is genuinely confessed and repented of, there is no more need for pretending to be someone we are not; no more fear, deceit and shame; no more condemnation. Who is it that condemns us? Ourselves? Our conscience? Our enemy (Satan)? All of the above. But not God! God calls us to confess our sins (secrets) and be free of condemnation.

"There is therefore now no condemnation for those who are in Christ Jesus" (Romans 8:1). Those who are in Christ Jesus keep short accounts. True healing can occur when we are willing to confess our secrets and unburden ourselves to God and those close to us. Once secrets are exposed, Satan can no longer use them against us. The power of secrets implodes once they are confessed.

Two personal stories help to illustrate many of the above points.

My name is Connie and I am a prescription drug addict. It feels so good to say that! You see, I was addicted for many years and no one knew. I was very functional, or so I thought. I had always found drugs a comfort but when I began to use my daughter's IV Dilaudid, I soon got myself into deep waters. Dilaudid is a drug that is a very potent pain killer. Yes, I actually started shooting it into myself. I increased the dosage very fast and soon was taking so much that there was no way I could stop without medical intervention. I couldn't tell anybody what I was doing. I was so ashamed and so full of guilt. I was teaching others about the Lord while I was dying inside. I slowly started dropping out of everything and began to hide out at home. I couldn't read my Bible or pray. My life was spiraling out of control. This secret I was carrying was so huge I was literally bent over from the weight. Then, just before Christmas, I overdosed and almost died. I lied to the people in the hospital and they had no idea what they were dealing with. I spent three days in ICU and it is a miracle that I lived. I continued to shoot up when I got home and that went on for another four months; then I got caught. My husband found my drugs and he laid it out in no uncertain terms. I would go to rehab and get the help I needed. I was numb as I got on a plane after almost being arrested for carrying my syringes. I went to detoxification and then to rehab. It was there that I began to understand that I really was an addict and I began to experience the amazing feeling of freedom that was only to grow as I came clean with my Savior and my family and myself. What a weight was lifted off of me and I began to see the incredible bondage that secrets had caused in my life. Today, I am free of drugs and work every day at being honest with my Lord, my friends and family and myself. There is no other way to live! To God be the Glory![152]

A well-respected man was arrested by federal agents and accused of being involved with child pornography. Although full of shame, uncertainty, humiliation and pain, the man also described that day in the following terms: "The day I was arrested was the best day of my life."

Why? Because no longer did he have to hide; no longer did he have to pretend to be someone he was not; no longer did he have to fear that someone would catch him. Now, he could begin the process of healing.

Detecting Children's Secrets

We need to listen and watch for clues that children might be harboring secrets. Parenting sometimes requires a lot of intuition. If we notice that the behavior of our children suddenly changes, or if we suspect that they are being evasive, it's time to question them. "Do you have something you need to tell me?" Or, "You seem quite angry lately. What's going on?" They may not answer immediately, but provide lots of opportunities to be alone with that child. Remind them that when they have something on their heart you want to be able to work it out with them. Be certain that you make time to be alone with that child, with lots of quiet time, time for them to engage with you. For example, when in the car keep the radio off, ear buds out of ears and distractions to a minimum.

Don't allow children to be surly and uncommunicative. Don't dismiss too easily a change in behavior as just a phase. If necessary, parents need to push into their children's lives. Keep asking questions, not confrontationally, but letting them know that you suspect something is troubling them.

Being real and honest takes the power out of secrets.

In the section on pornography the stories of two adolescents were told, both of whom wanted to confess a secret pornography addiction. Confession of any secret is hard to do and one tends to test the waters by first circling around the real issue. Listen carefully: what they comment on may be a loaded comment. One of these boys complained to his mother about all the pop-ups which were suddenly plaguing his computer. This needed to be investigated: was he doing something which encouraged such pop-ups? Had he been looking at sites that triggered the pop-ups? Don't let seemingly innocent comments go. Follow up and find out what thoughts, feelings and experiences are behind the comments.

The other young man, in a conversation with one of his parents about pornography, said with great disgust: "I can't believe what's on the Internet." (See full story in Chapter 7.) Don't let a comment such as this go. Follow up. How does he know about such abhorrent things displayed on the Internet? Ask, "Do you have a problem in this area?"

Living Openly in Families

It is a wise parent who doesn't allow children to hole up in their room for long periods of time. Family life is community life and living in view of one another greatly reduces the possibility of secretive behavior. It is a good idea to have computers situated in family areas, lessening the opportunity to view destructive material in private. It is also smart to set guidelines for cell phone use. Encourage as much family living in the open as possible.

One wise mother called her college-aged daughter from 3,000 miles away to ask what was troubling her. Even from such a distance that mother knew something was wrong. She explained that she just had a sense that her daughter was really struggling with some life issues. The mom was right— her daughter was struggling and desperately needed to talk some things out.

Moms, particularly, are naturals at this kind of intuition. Don't dismiss such nudges; follow up and keep pushing until your children talk. You're doing the wash and find a note in your teen's pocket or backpack. Should you read it? It is not a violation of privacy to read that note; it may well alert you to some issue where they need help.

Families should expect that plans be shared, the where, what, when and with whom involved in the activities of each family member. That is:

➢ Where are you going?

➢ What are you planning?

➢ When will you be home?

➢ Whom are you going with?

This kind of open living greatly increases the sense of community and emphasizes the point that your family lives interdependent lives.

All too often one may hear a parent say, "I don't want to know" or "I wouldn't want to know what my kids are doing." If a parent doesn't want to know, where is the help for our teens? An attitude such as this condemns our children to lonely battles and increasingly difficult consequences, consequences which have to be faced alone. It gives a clear signal of parental disinterest and encourages secrets. Being real and honest, on the other hand, takes the power out of secrets. A mantra of one wise mom to her children: "If you have to do it in secret, it's just wrong."

Chapter 19

MARITAL MODELING

Modeling healthy marriages for our children is as important as what we talk about because we know that a picture is worth a thousand words. One of the richest ways to teach our children is through modeling. We can say a lot of things to them, but what they see is what they are apt to believe. Do our actions fit our words?

Fights

Some parents try to hide disagreements and fights from their children, thinking that they only want their children to see the positive in their relationship. Children are aware of the emotional tenor in our homes and, though we may think we are hiding our anger toward our spouse, kids seem to know when there is disagreement.

One family was on an extended car/camping trip so the entire family was always together. The parents disagreed about something, grew angrier and angrier, and finally refused to talk or even look at each other. The air was heavy with tension. Until this time the children had not been that physically close to their parents when they were fighting. Soon they began to worry that their parents were going to get a divorce. That evening in the kids' tent, divorce was a serious subject of discussion. After all, they knew that when couples didn't get along, divorce was often the result.

Sometime during the next day it became clear that the parents were back in communication and the storm had passed. But the children were never given an explanation nor any teaching on what you do when you have disagreements. They never learned how to fight fairly. Those children entered their marriages with the example of strong, silent, don't-speak-to-each-other fighting. They didn't know how to talk things out. The only thing they knew was to clam up when faced with disagreements, wait it out until one or the other got tired of the silence, then sweep the issue under the carpet and put it away—until the next time. In this manner a lot of anger and hurt feelings get stored up, all of which come out in subsequent fights.

One of the adages of "Marriage Encounter," a workshop designed to make good marriages better, is "don't throw dirty laundry." The idea behind this? When we don't deal with issues but sweep them under the carpet, we store up an ever-increasing arsenal of hurts and wounds that get aired each time we're angry. Words such as "always" or "never" pack a wallop of past history. Whereas, if we deal with each thing, each disagreement, we can put it away for good and it does not need to reemerge the next time.

Children can learn a lot about how to fight by watching their parents. But more than learning how to fight, they learn how to make peace, how to resolve issues which cause disagreements. If parents hide their fights from their children, how will children learn how to make up? Where two or three are gathered together, disagreements will result. The closer the relationship, the greater the probability of occasional arguments, disagreements and fights.

I thought I had it down. I had lived with roommates successfully and with little friction for ten years. I knew how to get along. I considered arguments, disagreements and fights to be childish. I thought I had grown up and was well past all of that. I expected the same smooth sailing in my marriage. What a wakeup call I had coming! It was several months into our marriage when we had our first fight. It started as a simple difference of opinion and escalated from that point. I couldn't believe the myriad of childish feelings I had. I didn't know what to do with these feelings and thought something was wrong with me. I had some growing up to do and a lot to learn.

Help children to understand that those who love each other don't always get along. Don't try to shield them from all of your disagreements, arguments or fights. If they are aware of your altercations that's fine, but see that they are also aware of the steps you take to attain peace and return to normal, loving relations. If they don't see you fight, they won't see you make up, and they will assume that adults always get along.

Affection

Children love to see affection demonstrated between their parents. They love to see their parents holding hands. Often, when children are young and husband and wife hug each other, children want to be part of that hug and the hug soon morphs into a group hug. They may even pull up a chair so they can be on a more equal plane with their parents; they want to be part of this display of affection. A deep sense of security results when children see affection modeled between their parents, so don't be shy about modeling appropriate (non-bedroom) affection in your home. Your children see a constant stream of non-married affection modeled at school, in movies, in public, almost anywhere. How much do they see from you? Good, healthy modeling of married affection gives children a view of what to emulate and assures them of their parents' attraction to each other.

> *A survey among college students revealed that many of them couldn't imagine their parents having sex.*

Josh McDowell—a Christian apologist, evangelist and writer who has written extensively about sex, purity and marriage—shares: "Often young people grow up without an awareness that their parents are sexually attracted to each other. A survey among college students revealed that many of them couldn't imagine their parents having sex."[153]

Following are three stories in which youth model a good understanding and healthy awareness of their parents' sexual love for one another.

In one family, 14-year-old Peter asked his mother what the reason was for the candle beside his parents' bed. He asked the question in such a way that his mom was pretty sure he knew the answer. He teasingly added, "Are you afraid that if the electricity goes out you will be scared?"

"No," she answered, smiling. "We light that when your dad and I make love." Apparently Peter told this to his slightly younger sister and, not many days later when kids and mom were together, one asked,

"So, did you light your candle last night?"

Another family was traveling on vacation (mom, dad and adolescent children). For two weeks they had shared sleeping space in one room. The last night the parents had a separate room. The family was alone in the dining room the next morning when, over breakfast, one of the children asked their parents,

"Did you two go right to sleep last night?" The questioner clearly thought otherwise.

"No," replied the father with a twinkle in his eyes.

"I know you didn't," the teen continued, "because we saw your light under the door. We knocked but you didn't answer."

Warmth, closeness and a sure sense of joy were shared by that family through the conversation.

One day, a high school student came home and said to his mother,

"I hear you and dad were at the grocery store at 11 last night."

His parents had been in the market late the night before to buy Advil and condoms. When they first entered the store five checkers were available; by the time they checked out only one remained. The mom knew that the remaining cashier was an acquaintance and classmate of their son's.

With mock horror the mom asked, "She didn't…?"

"Yes, she did, and she told me what you bought."

"What did you say to her?" Asked his mom, curious.

"So, my parents have sex," he replied. "Don't yours?"

Freedom, delight and joy can be shared in families where sex is an open and dignified topic.

You Can Do It !

Chapter 20

A PICTURE OF HOPE

You can do it! *You* can talk to your children about sex and sexuality. Remember that if you can talk about sex, you can talk about anything. Start talking when your children are young and talk regularly. Build a close, caring, trusting relationship. As they get older, move the conversation from body parts and mechanics to God's purpose in giving this wonderful, joy-filled, good gift of sex.

But What if Our Youth "Blow It"?

What if, after talking early and often, persevering throughout the years of your children's growing up, and forming solid relationships with them, your son or daughter succumbs to the pressure and goes the way of the world? What do we do?

When John Rogers (1570-1636) first went up to Emmanuel College, Cambridge, as a student in February 1588, he proved to be a complete waste. His way was being paid by his uncle, the well-known Puritan preacher Richard Rogers (1551-1618), but John sold all of his books so as to spend the proceeds on various sinful activities. Not surprisingly, Emmanuel College, a hotbed of Puritan theology and piety, asked John to leave. Richard Rogers' wife convinced her husband to give the young man another chance. So John went up again to Cambridge, only to prove the profligate once more, again selling his books and squandering money on his vices. His uncle would have washed his hands of him, but yielding to the entreaties of his wife, Richard sent John to Cambridge a third time. This time things proved quite different, as a longsuffering God saved the young man.[154]

Rogers went on to be a very powerful preacher, sometimes preaching to 1,200 people. Some would come from 60 miles away just to hear him preach.[155]

One can also think of Jesus' words to Peter just before He was crucified. He told Peter that he would deny that he knew Jesus three times. But Jesus went on to tell him, "but I have prayed for you.... And when you have turned again, strengthen your brothers" (Luke 22:32). In other words, Peter, you're going to blow it big time, but when you understand what I have done to forgive you, then get back on the path.

We, too, need to pray earnestly for our wayward young people, praying that they, like John Rogers and Peter, will turn, get back on their feet and continue along the "narrow road."

Derek Redmond pulled a hamstring muscle and collapsed at the Barcelona 1992 Summer Olympic Games:

With the crush of disappointment and the piercing agony of pain written on his face, he struggled to get to his feet. Olympic officials hurried to help him off the track. But with tears rolling down his face, he shoved them aside. Suddenly all of us watching at home, and most of the people in the crowd, could see what he was doing. He was going to finish the race! Years of training, hard work, and sacrifice had disintegrated on that hot Barcelona afternoon, but he was resolved to finish the race.

The pain was so great he stumbled, hopped, and hobbled. It looked for a while as if there was no physical way he could go on. The race was long over when the crowd began to cheer for Derek. Even with their encouragement, it appeared he just couldn't do it. Terrifying pain was overcoming the will to go on.

Then an older man illegally broke through the ranks of people around the track. The man walked right up to Derek Redmond and grabbed him around the chest. Derek threw his arm over the man's shoulder.

That was no official trying to get Derek off the track. That man was trying to help a courageous determined athlete complete the race.

The man was Derek Redmond's father.

Still in anguish, Derek completed the race to the standing ovation of all in the stadium.

A loser?

Not in my eyes.

Nor, I'm sure, in the eyes of his father.[156]

What do we do if our children "fall"? We continue to love them. Don't give up on them. Don't cast them aside. Don't condemn them. Rather, love them. Listen to them, pray for them, continue to pursue them. Encourage them to admit what they've done. Keep reminding them of their need for repentance. Help them back into the race so they can finish the course.

Chapter 21

CONCLUSION

"Aim at Heaven and you will get Earth 'thrown in': aim at Earth and you will get neither." C.S. Lewis[157]

Parents, you have a choice. There are three ways you can relate with your children about this topic of sex and sexuality:

1. Anything Goes

"Whatever makes you happy," a segment of parents advise. "Just leave me out of it." You can choose to be silent on the subject of sex. In your silence you will, in essence, give your children over to the culture, to schools, peers and the media to be educated. These sources will probably convince them that anything goes—whatever makes them happy, do it.

2. Proscription: "No's" and Fears

You could also parent by proscription, giving them an ever-increasing number of rules to abide by—"Don't do this," "Don't do that," "You'd better be home by (time), or..."—filling them with fears of the dangers of sex and talking as if sex is dirty and a bad thing which causes any number of ills and pains. This is parenting without relationship and "rules without relationship lead to rebellion."[158] The more legalistic we are, the greater the chance that our kids will rebel.

3. Point Them Toward the Joy Set Before Them

Or, talking early and often, you can set before them the joy that God intended. You can encourage their movement from external monitoring to internal monitoring as they are more and more able to articulate, and then act on, their knowledge of the good, the beautiful and the lovely. Much effort and constant vigilance are necessary. Is it worth it? I say, Yes!

One day, after much preparation and a great deal of anticipation, you will look down the aisle at your daughter standing at the back of the church on the arm of her father, waiting to be given in marriage to her love, her groom. Or, you'll look at the front of the church where your son stands with tears in his eyes, gazing upon the beauty and purity of his bride, the one that he is about to begin loving as Christ loves His church. And because of God's love and mercy, they are both without spot or wrinkle.

Aim at Heaven

Pressure to conform to worldly standards bombards today's parents and teens from every direction. Advertisers want us to believe that the world runs on sex. Academia tries to convince us that further research from medical science will eliminate our problems. Educators claim that kids will protect themselves properly and self-monitor with enough education. Once they are adolescents, we are told, we should just trust them. And many voices are telling parents not to stifle their children with ancient proscriptions. But, no matter what the protections, no matter what the education, no condom exists for the heart or the spirit.

Parents, arm your children with hope, that sure knowledge that we were created for God and by God and we are bound for glory. One day our bodies will be resurrected—in a renewed body meaningfully related to our present bodies—and we will be with Him forever. "You are not your own, for you were bought with a price. So glorify God in your body" (1 Corinthians 6:19b-20).

All those who love the Lord Jesus Christ await our ultimate bridegroom: "The Spirit and the Bride say, 'Come.' And let the one who hears say, 'Come.' And let the one who is thirsty come; let the one who desires take the water of life without price" (Revelation 22:17).

Our task as Christian parents is hard and sometimes lonely work requiring dogged persistence. Yet the results of encouraging our children to become who God made them, of training them up in righteousness and teaching them God's truth, are worth it!

APPENDIX

Creative Dating Ideas

1. Buy a puzzle to work on when you're bored or there's rainy weather.

2. Go to the public library and write a report of what was happening in the world on the day you were born. (Yes, I know you can do this on the Web at home, but the library gives you a public place to go).

3. Make dinner using only ingredients which start with the following letters: A, B, C, P, R, and T.

4. Go to a sports event with a recording device and do one of two things: interview a player or narrate a play-by-play of an inning.

5. Go bowling with parents—the ones with the worst scores have to make dinner for all the rest.

6. Pick a bouquet of wild flowers and take them to a "shut in."

7. Take your favorite little kids to a maize maze.

8. Go to the store, buy and eat a popsicle. Now you have popsicle sticks. Use these to attach the main sail onto two boats which you will construct. Take these boats to a river. Take along an impartial judge, or several, and race your boats: best 3 out of 5 wins.

9. Go to a beautiful place. Take a picture of the place and write a poem—either individually or together (or you could compose a song.)

10. Go with a group and divide up into at least two groups. Go to a beautiful place (agreed upon before). Each group take a picture of the place then ask an impartial judge(s) to decide the best picture. The group that wins buys ice cream for the others (if not too big a group).

11. Go to a pond after dark. Catch a frog. Make a video of a girl kissing the frog (well, sort of). Using the video editing equipment morph that frog into a handsome prince!

12. Invite a group to have a picnic and bonfire on the beach.

13. Go to a play with parents.

14. Play a game of Live Clue.

15. Go biking to a prearranged place.

16. Plan a hike with some of the "older" people you know.

17. Bake cookies and have tea with someone in the community who might be lonely.

18. Have a dinner with your families. Draw names and pretend you are that person throughout the meal.

19. Go on a scavenger hunt.

20. Pick a short distance on one of the roads around you and clean up all trash, plastic bags, etc.

21. With at least 4 people, divide into groups. Each group decide on a theme. Find creative ways to take pictures to document your theme. Agree on a time when all groups will meet at the home of one of the group members and share each group's series of pictures. Try to guess the theme.

22. Go to the airport, mall or some other busy place and people watch.

23. With a small amount of money ($5 or $10) go to a mall and buy as many things as possible. This would be fun in a group, too, to see which group was able to buy the most things.

24. Have a progressive dinner by "begging" at homes of friends, neighbors or, if brave—any home.

25. Watch a movie without sound—come up with dialogue and sound/music.

1. Kristine Napier, *The Power of Abstinence* (Avon Books, 1996), 9.

2. "Ten Tips for Parents to Help Their Children Avoid Pregnancy," *The National Campaign to Prevent Teen and Unplanned Pregnancy*, accessed July 23, 2012, 7, www.thenationalcampaign.org/resources/pdf/pubs/10Tips_final.pdf.

3. Sylvia Wood, "School Playground 'Rape Tag' Sparks Concern," *U.S. News*, February 2, 2012, Web.

4. "Sexually Transmitted Infections," *WHO*, August 2011, 1, http://www.who.int/mediacentre/factsheets/fs110/en/.

5. "Sexually Transmitted Diseases (STDs)," *Planned Parenthood*, accessed July 23, 2012, http://www.plannedparenthood.org/health-topics/stds-hiv-safer-sex-101.htm.

6. Louise Sloan, "Who's Most at Risk for STDs?," *Health.com*, last updated October 16, 2008, http://www.health.com/health/article/print/0,,20411478,00.html.

7. David T. Ellwood and Christopher Jencks, "The Spread of Single-Parent Families in the United States since 1960," *Harvard University*, February 2004, http://web.lemoyne.edu/~ridzifm/fmridzi_files/maxwell_school/Soc%20281%20files/Policy%20Conference/ellwood-jencks.pdf.

8. "Children in Single-Parent Families by Race," *Annie E. Casey Foundation*, accessed July 23, 2012, http://datacenter.kidscount.org/data/acrossstates/Rankings.aspx?ind=107.

9. Carmen Solomon-Fears, "CRS Report to Congress, Nonmarital Childbearing: Trends, Reasons, and Public Policy Interventions," *Congressional Research Service*, November 20, 2008, 5, http://www.fas.org/sgp/crs/misc/RL34756.pdf.

10. Joyce A. Martin, et al., *National Vital Statistics Report*, 60:1, November 3, 2011, 8, http://www.cdc.gov/nchs/data/nvsr/nvsr60/nvsr60_01.pdf.

11. Sheetal Malhotra, "Impact of the Sexual Revolution: Consequences of Risky Sexual Behaviors," *Journal of American Physicians and Surgeons* 13:3 (2008): 88.

12. D.P. Orr, M. Beiter, and G. Ingersoll, "Premature Sexual Activity as an Indicator of Psychosocial Risk," *Pediatrics* 87:2 (1991): 141-47.

13. "Facts and Figures. National Statistics," *American Foundation for Suicide Prevention*, 2010, http://www.afsp.org/index.cfm?fuseaction=home.viewpage&page_id=050fea9f-b064-4092-b1135c3a70de1fda.

14. "Teen Suicide Statistics," *Teen Depression,* April 25, 2012, http://www.teendepression.org/related/teen-suicide-statistics/.

15. See Endnote 14.

16. "Pornography Statistics," *Enough Is Enough*, 2009-2010, http://www.internetsafety101.org/Pornographystatistics.htm.

17. See Endnote 16.

18. Jason S. Carroll, et al., "Generation XXX: Pornography Acceptance and Use Among Emerging Adults," *Journal of Adolescent Research* 23:23 (2008): 6-30, abstract, http://jar.sagepub.com/content/23/1/6.

19. *Sesame Street Parents,* 1998.

20. Josh McDowel, "Helping Your Teen Say No to Sex," *Focus on the Family* (Feb. 1989): 4.

21. Ravi Zacharias, *Deliver Us From Evil* (Nashville, Tennessee: Thomas Nelson Inc., 1996), 64. All rights reserved. Reprinted by permission.

22. Kimberly Erickson, "Sexual Activity and Youth," *The Institute for Youth Development*, Oct. 1998, 7, http://www.youthdevelopment.org/download/sex.pdf.

23. N.L. Leland, and R.P. Barth, "Characteristics of Adolescents Who Have Attempted to Avoid HIV and Who Have Communicated with Parents About Sex," *Journal of Adolescent Research* 8:1 (1993), 71.

24. Anne Nesbit, "Learning About Myself and Others: A Program in the Study of Human Sexuality for Parents and Children Together: Grades 1 thru 6," Pittsfield, MA.

25. Lynda Madaras, *The What's Happening to My Body? Book for Girls,* 3rd rev. ed. (Newmarket Press, 2001), xxiv. Used by permission.

26. M.D. Resnick, et al., "Protecting Adolescents from Harm: Findings from the National Longitudinal Study on Adolescent Health," *JAMA* 278:10 (1997), 823-32.

27. "It's a Guy Thing: Boys, Young Men, and Teen Pregnancy Prevention," The *National Campaign to Prevent Teen Pregnancy,* Feb. 2006, 148, http://www.thenationalcampaign.org/resources/pdf/pubs/Guy_Thing.pdf.

28. Stephanie J. Ventura and Brady E. Hamilton, "U.S. Teenage Birth Rate Resumes Decline," *CDC,* February 2011, http://www.cdc.gov/nchs/data/databriefs/db58.htm.

29. J.C. Abma, C.M. Martinez, W.D. Mosher, and B.S. Dawson, "Teenagers in the United States: Sexual Activity, Contraceptive Use, and Childbearing," *CDC,* October 2011, 29, http://www.cdc.gov/nchs/data/series/sr_23/sr23_031.pdf.

30. See Endnote 6.

31. See Endnote 6.

32. "U.S. Teen Sexual Activity," *Kaiser Family Foundation* Publication #3040-02, (Jan. 2005), 2, http://www.kff.org/womenshealth/upload/3040-05-2.pdf.

33. Cal Thomas, "Schools for Scandal: A Failing Grade for Sex and the Single-Minded Culture," *Pittsburgh Post Gazette,* Oct. 2, 1997, http://news.google.com/newspapers?nid=19971002&id=adRRAAAAIBAJ&sjid=yW8DAAAAIBA&pg=4258,1084648.

34. Will Dunham, "CDC Says 1.1 Million Americans Infected with HIV," *Reuters*, October 2, 2008, http://www.reuters.com/article/2008/10/02/us-aids-usa-idUSTRE49166C20081002.

35. Frederica Mathewes-Green, *Real Choices: Listening to Women; Looking for Alternatives to Abortion* (Ben Lomond, CA: Acorn Publishing, 1997), 11.

36. David C. Reardon, *The Jericho Plan: Breaking down the Walls Which Prevent Post-Abortion Healing* (Springfield, IL: Acorn Publishing, 1996).

37. Dennis Rainey, "Beyond Abstinence: Helping Your Teen Stay Pure," *FamilyLife Today,* Audio Tape Series.

38. Jacqueline Nowotny, "A Look into the Consequences of Sex for Gordon Students," *The Tartan* (Wenham, MA), 7 May 2010.

39. Vicki Courtney, *5 Conversations You Must Have with Your Daughter* (Nashville, Tennessee: B & H Publishing, 2008), 145-46. Used by permission.

40. *Reader's Digest*, Feb. 1993, 83.

41. Jane Graver, *How You Are Changing* (St. Louis, MO: Concordia Publishing House, 1995), 6.

42. Two suggestions of age-appropriate series on sexual development: *God's Design for Sex: A Four Book Series* (Colorado Springs, CO: Navpress, 1995); *Learning About Sex: A Series for the Christian Family* (St. Louis, MO: Concordia Publishing House, 2008).

43. *God's Design for Sex*. Also: *Learning About Sex*.

44. David Freeman, "Men's Health," *WebMD*, September 27, 2012, http://men.webmd.com/features/male-breast-enlargement-gynecomastia.

45. See Endnote 3.

46. Dennis Rainey and Barbara Rainey, *Passport2Purity® Getaway Kit by FamilyLife, Version 3* (2012).

47. *The Miracle of Life*, Time-Life Video (1986), DVD.

48. Richard Bimler, *Sex and the New You* (Saint Louis, MO: Concordia Publishing House, 1998), 53.

49 Maggie Gallagher, "The Divorce Paradox," *The Manila Times.Net*, August 18, 2011, Web.

50. Anjani Chandra, William D. Mosher, and Casey Copen, "Sexual Behavior, Sexual Attraction, and Sexual Identity in the United States: Data From the 2006-2008 National Survey of Family Growth," *CDC National Health Statistics Report*, March 3, 2011, http://www.cdc.gov/nchs/data/nhsr/nhsr036.pdf.

51. Martin Hallett, quoted in Wesley Hill, *Washed and Waiting:* (Grand Rapids, MI: Zondervan, 2010), 16.

52. Wesley Hill, *Washed and Waiting* (Grand Rapids, MI: Zondervan, 2010), 13.

53. Hill, *Washed and Waiting,* 15.

54. Erickson, "Sexual Activity and Youth," 3.

55. Kathleen Doheny, "Many Teen Girls Mistakenly Think HPV Vaccines Cut Risk for All STDs," *Health* Day, last updated January 5, 2012, http://consumer.healthday.com/Article.asp?AID=660419.

56. Erickson, "Sexual Activity and Youth," 4.

57. Reardon, *The Jericho Plan,* 44.

58. Stephen Marche, "Is Facebook Making Us Lonely?" *The Atlantic*, May 2012, http://www.theatlantic.com/magazine/archive/2012/05/is-facebook-making-us-lonely/308930/.

59. "Pornography Research," *Josh McDowell Ministry*, accessed April 9, 2012, 12, http://www.just1clickaway.org/objects/Pornography Research_ALL_324113122.pdf.

60. "Pornography Research," 15.

61. "Pornography Research," 16.

62. "Pornography Research," 21.

63. "Pornography Research," 23.

64. "Pornography Research," 3.

65. "Pornography Research," 52.

66. "Pornography Research," 19.

67. "Pornography Research," 4.

68. "Pornography Research," 30.

69. "Pornography Research," 37.

70. "Pornography Research," 35.

71. "Pornography Research," 44.

72. "Pornography Research," 43.

73. "Pornography Research," 2.

74. "Pornography Research," 34.

75. "Pornography Research," 36.

76. "Pornography Research," 4, 46.

77. "Pornography Research," 38.

78. See Endnote 68.

79. See Endnote 70.

80. See Endnote 70.

81. "Pornography Research," 45.

82. See Endnote 80.

83. See Endnote 64.

84. "Pornography Research," 53.

85. See Endnote 63.

86. "Pornography Research," 2, 43.

87. Debra Bradley Ruder, "The Teen Brain," *Harvard Magazine*, Sept.-Oct. 2008, http://harvardmag.com/pdf/2008/09-pdfs/0908-8.pdf.

88. Barbara Cooke, "The Teenage Brain," *Family Education,* accessed July 25, 2012, http://life.familyeducation.com/teen/growth-and-development/36499.html.

89. "Two Teen Girls Hit by Car While Sunbathing in the Road," *U.S. News*, April 30, 2012, http://usnews.nbcnews.com/_news/2012/04/30/11471297-two-teen-girls-hit-by-car-while-sunbathing-in-the-road?lite.

90. "Car Surfing: A Deadly Trend," *CBS News*, October 16, 2010, http://www.cbsnews.com/2100-18563_162-6965240.html.

91. Cooke, "The Teenage Brain."

92. Ruder, "The Teen Brain," 10.

93. Jeffrey Jensen Arnett, "Emerging Adulthood: A Theory of Development from the Late Teens through the Twenties," *American Psychologist* 55:5 (2000): 469-80.

94. Cheryl Crawford, "Will Your Kids Have Faith After High School?," *Youth Symposium, Gordon College* (Wenham, MA), October 2010, Lecture.

95. Arnett, "Emerging Adulthood," 473.

96. Alex Harris, and Brett Harris, *Do Hard Things: A Teenage Rebellion against Low Expectations* (Colorado Springs, CO: Multnomah, 2008), 33.

97. Linda Burgess Chamberlain, "The Amazing Adolescent Brain: What Every Educator, Youth-Serving Professional, and Healthcare Provider Needs to Know," *Institute for Safe Families*, accessed July 25, 2012, 1, http://www.multiplyingconnections.org/sites/default/files/ Teen%20Provider%20article%20(2)_0.pdf.

98. Hill, *Washed and Waiting,* 7.

99. Josh McDowell and Dick Day, *Why Wait?: What You Need to Know about the Teen Sexuality Crisis* (San Bernardino, CA: Here's Life, 1987), 79.

100. Joshua Harris, *I Kissed Dating Goodbye* (Sisters, OR: Multnomah Publishers, 1997), 71.

101. Richard Phillips, "No Room for Indifference," *Tabletalk Magazine, Ligonier Ministries,* July 2010.

102. McDowell, *Why Wait?*, 386.

103. David Carder, *Close Calls: What Adulterers Want You to Know about Protecting Your Marriage* (Chicago, IL: Northfield Publishing, 2008), 23.

104. Mike Nagel, "Just 221 Days from Now, My Commitment to Virginity Will Be over," *Boston Globe,* October 26, 2008.

105. Ravi Zacharias, *Deliver Us From Evil* (Nashville, Tennessee: Thomas Nelson Inc., 1996), 14-15. All rights reserved. Reprinted by permission.

106. Dawson McAllister, *Preparing Your Teenager for Sexuality: A Discussion Manual* (Irving, TX: Shepherd Ministries, 1988), 35.

107. Dawson McAllister, *Preparing Your Teenager for Sexuality,* VHS Tape C, Sessions 5-6 (God the Great Protector/Practical Steps to Purity), 1988.

108. See Endnote 93.

109. See Endnote 93.

110. "College Drinking, What It Is, and What To Do About It: A Review of the State of the Science," *Journal of Studies on Alcohol Supplement* 14 (March 2002): 5, http://www.collegedrinkingprevention.gov/media/Journal/001_022.pdf.

111. H. Wechsler, et al., "Underage College Students' Drinking Behavior, Access to Alcohol, and the Influence of Deterrence Policies: Findings from the Harvard School of Public Health College Alcohol Study," *Journal of American College Health* 50:5 (March 2002): 223-236.

112. "Facts About Youth and Alcohol," *American Medical Association*, October 7, 2012, http://www.ama-assn.org/ama/pub/ physician-resources/public-health/promoting-healthy-lifestyles/alcohol-other-drug-abuse/facts-about-youth-alcohol.page.

113. "Facts About Youth and Alcohol."

114. See Endnote 23.

115. John S Santelli, et al., "Multiple Sexual Partners Among U.S. Adolescents and Young Adults," *Family Planning Perspectives* 30:6 (Nov./Dec. 1998): 273.

116. See Endnote 93.

117. Arnett, "Emerging Adulthood," 473.

118. "Dictionary, Encyclopedia and Thesaurus," *The Free Dictionary*, Farlex, accessed August 2, 2012, http://www.thefree dictionary.com/.

119. Zachary Hannah. Used by permission.

120. Patsy G. Lovell, "Hold Fast," *Focus on the Family,* October 1993, 14. Used by permission of the author.

121. McDowell, *Why Wait?,* 386.

122. Jerram Barrs, *Learning Evangelism from Jesus* (Wheaton, IL: Crossway, 2009), 174.

123. *Tabletalk Magazine*, Ligonier Ministries, August 26, 2010, 60.

124. "Sex Before Marriage (Over Time)," *Association of Religion Archives*, 1999, http://www.thearda.com/quickstats/qs_120_t.asp.

125. Matthew Henry, *Tabletalk Magazine,* Ligonier Ministries, September 27, 2010, 62.

126. Tim Keller, "Is There A Biblical Commandment Against Pre-Marital Sex?" Audio blog post, Questions and Answers, *Redeemer Presbyterian Church*, New York City, accessed June 27, 2012, http://download.redeemer.com/rpcsermons/QandA/Is_there_a_Biblical_commandment_against_pre-marital_sex.mp3.

127. Gordon P. Hugenberger, "Theology of the Pentateuch," Semlink #3.2.01, *Gordon-Conwell Theological Seminary* (South Hamilton, MA), 2006, Lecture.

128. Sheetal Malhotra, "Impact of the Sexual Revolution," 89.

129. Joe S. McIlhaney and Freda McKissic Bush, *Hooked: New Science on How Casual Sex Is Affecting Our Children* (Chicago, IL: Northfield Publishing, 2008), 63, 94.

130. Robert Rector and Kirk Johnson, "Teenage Sexual Abstinence and Academic Achievement," *The Heritage Foundation*, August 2005, 24, http://www.heritage.org/research/reports/2005/10/teenage-sexual-abstinence-and-academic-achievement.

131. Sheetal Malhotra, "Impact of the Sexual Revolution," 88.

132. Sheetal Malhotra, "Impact of the Sexual Revolution," 89.

133. P.B. Wilson, *Liberated Through Submission: God's Design for Freedom in All Relationships* (Eugene, OR: Harvest House Publishers, 1990), 152.

134. Dorington Little, "The Cross-Shaped Life," *First Congregational Church of Hamilton* (South Hamilton, MA), July 11, 2010, Sermon.

135. Little, "The Cross-Shaped Life.

136. *An Education*, dir. Lone Scherfig, perf. Carey Mulligan, Peter Sarsgaard, DVD, 2009.

137. See Endnote 125.

138. Bill Hendrick, "Benefits in Delaying Sex Until Marriage," *WebMD*, December 28, 2012, http://www.webmd.com/sex-relationships/news/20101227/theres-benefits-in-delaying-sex-until-marriage.

139. Hill, *Washed and Waiting,* 106.

140. See Endnote 124.

141. *Tabletalk Magazine*, Ligonier Ministries, June 2012, 62.

142. Adaptation of John 2:1-11.

143. Adaptation of John 8:1-11.

144. Adaptation of John 20.

145. "Couple Married 72 Years Dies Holding Hands," *msnbc.com*, updated October 19, 2011, http://www.ksee24.com/news/local/Couple-Married-72-Years-Dies-Holding-Hands-132201138.html.

146. Robertson McQuilkin, taken from *A Promise Kept* (Carol Stream, IL: Tyndale House Publishers), copyright © 1998, 2006, 18-19. Used by permission. All rights reserved.

147. Taken from the hymn "The Church's One Foundation," words by Samuel J. Stone.

148. Edwin G. Brown, "A Son's Point of View," *How to Talk to Your Teenager*, 1982, http://www.lds.org/braille/How_to_Talk_to_Your_Teenager.txt.

149. Corrie Ten Boom and Jamie Buckingham, *Tramp for the Lord* (Fort Washington, PA: Christian Literature Crusade, 1974), 116.

150. Matthew Henry as quoted in *Tabletalk Magazine,* Ligonier Ministries, Feb. 2012, 30.

151. *Tabletalk Magazine*, Ligonier Ministries, May 9, 2012, 42.

152. Connie Medak. Used by permission.

153. McDowell, *Why Wait?*, 384-385.

154. Michael A. G. Haykin, "A Boanerges and a Barnabas," *Tabletalk Magazine*, Ligonier Ministries, March 2012, 32-33.

155. "'Roaring John' Rogers (abt 1572-1636) of Dedham, Essex," accessed March 2012, http://rjohara.net/gen/rogers/jr-dnb.

156. Stephen A. Bly, excerpted from *Once a Parent, Always a Parent*, a Focus on the Family book published by Living Books, Copyright © 1993, 231-232. Used by permission.

157. C.S. Lewis, *The Joyful Christian* (Macmillan, 1977), 138.

158. McDowell, *Why Wait?,* 386.